# SWORDTAILS
# AND PLATIES

Dr. Herbert R. Axelrod
Mr. Lothar Wischnath

A beautiful red lyretail *Xiphophorus helleri*. An example of a swordtail in almost perfect condition. This is one of the many popular aquarium-bred fancy varieties of swordtail. Photo by L. Wischnath.

**ADDITIONAL PHOTOGRAPHY ACKNOWLEDGMENTS**

The following credits apply in addition to the acknowledgments listed with the captions accompanying photographs: SAM DUNTON, NYZS: page 24, middle. MANFRED K. MEYER: page 51, top photo in each column, third from top in left column; page 52, all photos except second photo from top in each column; page 53, all; page 54, all except second from top in left column; page 55, all except second from top in left column; page 58, all; page 73, bottom photo in right column and all except top in left column; page 76, all. K. D. KALLMANN: page 174, top. HORST LINKE: page 14, right row, topmost and lower two; page 51, bottom of left column, third from top in right column. HANS MAYLAND: page 54, second from top in left column; page 73, third from top in right column. DR. JOANNE NORTON: page 177, top. E. PÜRZL: page 73, top photo in each column. H. J. RICHTER: page 14, left column and second from top, right row; page 51, bottom right and second from top in each column. L. SEEGERS: page 52, second from top in right column; page 55, second from top in left column; page 73, second from top in right column. A. VAN DEN NIEUWENHUIZEN: page 144, top. LOTHAR WISCHNATH: page 18, second from top; page 52, second from top in left column; page 65, bottom; pages 68 and 69, all. GENE WOLFSHEIMER: page 155, bottom.

An example of the Berlin strain of *Xiphophorus helleri*. Photo by L. Wischnath.

# SWORDTAILS AND PLATIES

## Dr. Herbert R. Axelrod
## Mr. Lothar Wischnath

Distributed in the UNITED STATES by T.F.H. Publications, Inc., One T.F.H. Plaza, Neptune City, NJ 07753; in CANADA to the Pet Trade by H & L Pet Supplies Inc., 27 Kingston Crescent, Kitchener, Ontario N2B 2T6; Rolf C. Hagen Ltd., 3225 Sartelon Street, Montreal 382 Quebec; in CANADA to the Book Trade by Macmillan of Canada (A Division of Canada Publishing Corporation), 164 Commander Boulevard, Agincourt, Ontario M1S 3C7; in ENGLAND by T.F.H. Publications, PO Box 15, Waterlooville PO7 6BQ; in AUSTRALIA AND THE SOUTH PACIFIC by T.F.H. (Australia) Pty. Ltd., Box 149, Brookvale 2100 N.S.W., Australia; in NEW ZEALAND by Ross Haines & Son, Ltd., 82 D Elizabeth Knox Place, Panmure, Auckland, New Zealand; in the PHILIPPINES by Bio-Research, 5 Lippay Street, San Lorenzo Village, Makati, Rizal; in SOUTH AFRICA by Multipet Pty. Ltd., P.O. Box 35347, Northway, 4065, South Africa. Published by T.F.H. Publications, Inc. Manufactured in the United States of America by T.F.H. Publications, Inc.

# TABLE OF CONTENTS

A colorful platy
strain of
*Xiphophorus*
*maculatus*.
Photo by Dr. H.
Grier.

# INTRODUCTION

At the time of the provisional revision by Rosen, 1979, the genus *Xiphophorus* Heckel, 1848, popularly known as swordtails and platies, included fifteen species. Since that time it has been expanded by only one species: *Xiphophorus andersi* Meyer and Schartl, 1980. As yet undescribed are one representative from northern Mexico as well as two taxa from the Panuco basin. Moreover, the taxonomic placement of certain *Xiphophorus couchianus* forms from the vicinity of Monterrey remains unclear. There are also almost 100 different domestically bred varieties.

The genus *Xiphophorus* consists of species with and without swords. The swordlike elongations of varying length of the lower tail-fin rays found in males of these species led to the designation **swordtail**. Up until 1960 only the so-called swordtails belonged to the genus *Xiphophorus*. The previously independent genus *Platypoecilus* Günther, 1866, was made up of swordless fishes that are very closely related to the swordtails. This genus was synonymized by Rosen in 1960 and its members were then classified in the genus *Xiphophorus*. Fishes of the former genus *Platypoecilus* commonly continue to be called **platies**. In discussions of the species of the genus *Xiphophorus* one can therefore speak of *Xiphophorus* without swords and *Xiphophorus* with swords. In the following chapters we shall speak of both the sword-bearing and non sword-bearing wild forms and strains of *Xiphophorus*.

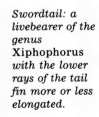

**This natural hybrid of *X. couchianus* X *X. variatus* was called *X. "roseni."* Photo by L. Wischnath.**

*Swordtail: a livebearer of the genus* Xiphophorus *with the lower rays of the tail fin more or less elongated.*

**This platy (*X. variatus*) is homozygous for a gene that reduces black pigment cells.**

**A red jet hi-fin swordtail (*X. helleri*) produced by Dr. Norton. Photo by Dr. H. R. Axelrod.**

*Color polymorphism: the occurrence of different color forms of individuals in a single species.*

**A young pair of hi-fin wagtail swordtails (*X. helleri*). Photo by R. Zukal.**

Some of the sword-bearing *Xiphophorus* species have a sword that can approach or even equal the male's remaining body length. Other species often have a barely visible sword only a few millimeters long, which is merely an elongation of the lower tail fin rays. With these species the swordlike elongation of the tail-fin rays plays a subordinate role in courtship. With the species with a long swordlike elongation of the tail fin, however, the sword is a very important component of the male's courtship behavior. During lightning-fast forward and backward swimming movements, with the body curved slightly to one side, the sword serves to encircle the courted female.

Due to the color polymorphism of the pigmentation, which is determined by macro- and micro-melanophores, fishes of the genus *Xiphophorus* have been used as experimental animals in genetic research for a fairly long time. Because of their tendency to develop inheritable melanomas they are also used in cancer research.

Its interesting zoogeography and systematics have made the genus *Xiphophorus* very popular with museum zoologists. The members of the genus *Xiphophorus* have a uniform, not very large range in Central America. On the Atlantic side it extends from Coahuila in northern Mexico as far south as Alta Verapaz in the central and western parts of Guatemala and Honduras. In the natural areas of occurrence of the species of the genus *Xiphophorus*, some live completely isolated from others. On the

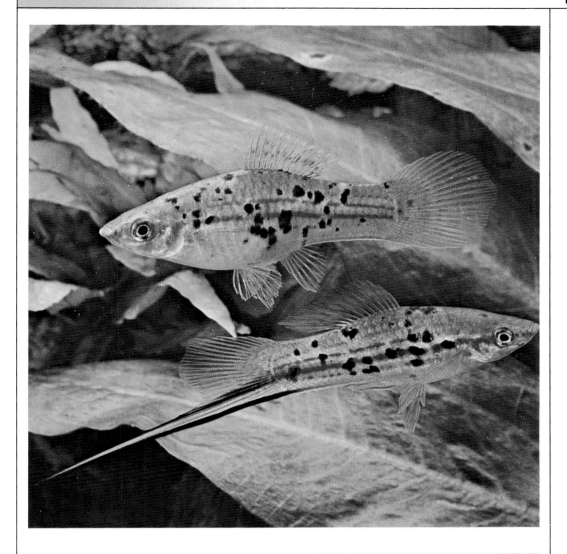

Black spots are commonly seen in wild populations of swordtails. Photo of *X. helleri* by H.-J. Richter.

*"During lightning-fast forward and backward swimming movements . . . the sword serves to encircle the courted female."*

The green swordtail is the original swordtail. This one is from Belize. Photo by A. van den Nieuwenhuizen.

*"The universally held view that* Xiphophorus *species predominantly live in medium-hard bodies of water is incorrect."*

*Biotope: an area of uniform environmental conditions and biota.*

A fancy strain of swordtail (*X. helleri*) called the red wag hi-fin tuxedo. Photo by B. Kahl.

other hand, other species live with one or two other species in one and the same stretch of water. In the natural habitats, whether in streams, rivers, or lakes, biotope boundries often are present, which are observed by the species or populations. For example, upper, middle, and lower courses of bodies of water may have different species or populations.

The universally held view that *Xiphophorus* species predominantly live in medium-hard bodies of water is incorrect. More than half of their natural environment consists of quite soft and very oxygen-rich water. Also worthy of note is that the species of the genus *Xiphophorus* for the most part occur in flowing bodies of water, some with very strong current. It is mostly in shallow rivers and streams or shallow sections of these bodies of water in which swordtails are found.

The **wild** forms of the genus *Xiphophorus* are in part rather difficult charges in the aquarium, and the most careful attention to water quality and feeding is required to maintain and spawn certain species. Under optimal conditions they can reach an age of from three to four years in the aquarium. The view often heard in aquarium circles that livebearers are, in general, begin-

Huasteca Canyon, Mexico, home of the Monterrey platy, *X. couchianus*. Photo by K. Kallman.

*Wild forms: individuals collected from their natural habitat as contrasted to domestic forms which have been raised in captivity and selectively bred for generations.*

A yellow variety of *Xiphophorus pygmaeus* from Rio Axtla. Photo by L. Wischnath.

ners' fishes has no basis in fact. Since certain species are already threatened in their natural ranges, the task of maintaining wild forms in aquaria is left to hobbyists. In the following detailed descriptions of the species and populations of the sword-bearing wild forms of the genus *Xiphophorus*, as well as their habitats, the water values will also be mentioned. These are average values from Mexico and the neighboring countries of Guatemala and Honduras.

*Xiphophorus helleri*, hobby strain.

*X. helleri*, Yucatan population.

*X. helleri*, Yucatan population.

*X. helleri*, hobby strain.

*X. helleri*, Rio del Reyon population.

*X. helleri*, Rio Sontecomapan population.

*X. helleri*, spotted hobby strain.

*X. helleri*, spotted form from Rio Blanco.

# THE WILD FORMS OF THE GENUS *XIPHOPHORUS*

*Xiphophorus cortezi* from Rio Panuco, Mexico. Photo by L. Wischnath.

*Natural hybrid: the resultant offspring when two different species interbreed in their natural habitat.*

# LISTING OF THE NAMES OF THE XIPHOPHORUS WILD FORMS

| SCIENTIFIC NAME | COMMON NAME |
|---|---|
| *Xiphophorus alvarezi* | Blue Swordtail |
| *Xiphophorus andersi* | Atoyac Swordtail Platy |
| *Xiphophorus clemenciae* | Yellow Swordtail |
| *Xiphophorus cortezi* | Cortez Swordtail |
| *Xiphophorus couchianus* | Monterrey Platy |
| *Xiphophorus evelynae* | Highland or Puebla Platy |
| *Xiphophorus gordoni* | Northern Platy |
| *Xiphophorus helleri* | Swordtail |
| *Xiphophorus* "kosszanderi" | Speckled Platy (natural hybrid) |
| *Xiphophorus maculatus* | Platy |
| *Xiphophorus milleri* | Catemaco Livebearer |
| *Xiphophorus montezumae* | Montezuma Swordtail |
| *Xiphophorus nigrensis* | Dwarf Helleri |
| *Xiphophorus pygmaeus* | Pygmy Swordtail |
| *Xiphophorus* "roseni" | Yellow Platy (natural hybrid) |
| *Xiphophorus signum* | Comma Swordtail |
| *Xiphophorus* sp. | Musquiz Platy |
| *Xiphophorus variatus* | Variegated Platy |
| *Xiphophorus xiphidium* | Swordtail Platy |

**Xiphophorus montezumae,** the Montezuma swordtail. Photo by L. Wischnath.

Wild pair of *Xiphophorus helleri* from Rio Blanco, Veracruz, Mexico. Photo by L. Wischnath.

A pair of spotted *Xiphophorus helleri* from Honduras. Photo by L. Wischnath.

A pair of wild swordtails, *Xiphophorus helleri*, from Rio San Juan. Photo by L. Wischnath.

A pair of 5-striped swordtails, *Xiphophorus helleri*, from Rio Sontecomapan. Photo by L. Wischnath.

An aquarium hybrid of *Xiphophorus helleri* from Catemaco and *X. helleri* from Rio Nautla.

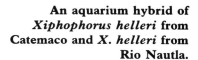

A naturally occurring albino *Xiphophorus helleri* from Rio Sontecomapan. Photo by L. Wischnath.

This wild male *Xiphophorus helleri* from Yucatan has a beautifully developed sword. Photo by L. Wischnath.

18

A wild pair of *Xiphophorus helleri* from Catemaco. Photo by L. Wischnath.

A pair of wild green swordtails, *Xiphophorus helleri*, from Rio Nautla. Photo by L. Wischnath.

A naturally occurring spotted swordtail, *Xiphophorus helleri*, from Rio Atoyac. Photo by L. Wischnath.

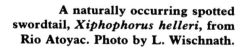

Another spotted male *Xiphophorus helleri*, but this one comes from Belize. Photo by L. Wischnath.

19

A spotted red male *Xiphophorus helleri* from Playa Vicente, Oaxaca. Photo by L. Wischnath.

This red male *Xiphophorus helleri* from Rio Atoyac, Veracruz, is unspotted. Photo by L. Wischnath.

An orange male *Xiphophorus helleri* from Rio Atoyac, Veracruz, with a few scattered spots. Photo by L. Wischnath.

# Concepts of Population and Variety

## Populations

Populations are organized collections of a species in a particular habitat. The members of populations are at least potentially capable of producing fertile offspring with one another. In this way, the unrestricted exchange of genetic material takes place. Not only does the entire population interrelate with its environment, the individual members also influence one another in many ways. To a considerable degree, the state of health; the development of characters, for example, colors in *Xiphophorus helleri*; the sex ratio; behavior; and the mortality of the individual members of the population can be dependent on population density. The most important phenomenon in biology—evolution and the creation of species that results from it—is also dependent on the grouping of organisms in different populations that are reproductively isolated from each other.

## Varieties

Varieties are groups of organisms within a species with shared inheritable variations from the original form that have no connection to geographic distribution, and which, therefore, do not represent geographic races or subspecies. Through captive breeding, in particular, varieties often were developed to extremes and designated as types, races, or sports. They have no status in the nomenclature, and their naming is not based on the rules of nomenclature. Varieties also occur within populations in the wild (for example, yellow males in *Xiphophorus pygmaeus*). In the aquarium hobby, varieties of livebearing toothcarps (Poeciliidae) are particularly well-known. Examples of varieties that have been produced in the aquarium include double swordtails as well as numerous sports of the platies *Xiphophorus maculatus* and *Xiphophorus variatus*.

*Xiphophorus cortezi from Rio Panuco. Photo by L. Wischnath.*

A handsomely colored male
*Xiphophorus evelynae* from Necaxa,
Mexico. Photo by L. Wischnath.

*Xiphophorus milleri* from Lake
Catemaco, Mexico. Photo by L.
Wischnath.

Facing page: Typical
appearance of a rocky stream
with fast moving water
somewhere in Mexico. In the
wild swordtails and platies
prefer to inhabit the deeper and
well-vegetated parts of fast-
water streams or rivers. Photo
by H.-J. Richter.

Male *Xiphophorus maculatus* from Rio Coatzacoalcos, Mexico. Photo by L. Wischnath.

*Xiphophorus milleri* from the vicinity of Catemaco, Veracruz, Mexico.

A pair of *Xiphophorus maculatus*, the male above. Photo by L. Wischnath.

A pair of *Xiphophorus maculatus* from Rio Papaloapan, Mexico. The black male is above. Photo by L. Wischnath.

Visual expression of the "nigra" gene. The female *X. maculatus* is from Belize, the males from the Rio Jamapa population. Photo by K. Kallman.

A pair of Jamapa platies from Rio Jamapa, Mexico. Photo by L. Wischnath.

# POPULATIONS AND VARIETIES OF WILD FORMS OF THE GENUS *XIPHOPHORUS*

| POPULATION NAME | COMMON NAME |
|---|---|
| *Xiphophorus helleri*, Rio Atoyac | Atoyac Swordtail |
| *Xiphophorus helleri*, Rio Atoyac | Red Atoyac Swordtail |
| *Xiphophorus helleri*, Belize River | Spotted Belize Swordtail |
| *Xiphophorus helleri*, Rio Blanco | Black-spotted Swordtail |
| *Xiphophorus helleri*, Laguna de Catemaco | Brass or Catemaco Swordtail |
| *Xiphophorus helleri*, Rio Sontecomapan | Sontecomapan Swordtail |
| *Xiphophorus helleri*, Rio del Reyon | Striped Swordtail |
| *Xiphophorus helleri*, Rio Nautla | Green Swordtail |
| *Xiphophorus helleri*, Rio Playa Vicente | Red and spotted Vicente Swordtail |
| *Xiphophorus helleri*, Yucatan | Yucatan Swordtail |
| *Xiphophorus nigrensis*, Rio Choy | Dwarf Swordtail |
| *Xiphophorus nigrensis*, Rio Coy | Dwarf Blue Swordtail |
| *Xiphophorus montezumae*, Rio Verde | Greater Montezuma Swordtail, original form |
| *Xiphophorus montezumae*, Rio Salto de Agua | Montezuma Swordtail |
| *Xiphophorus maculatus*, Rio Jamapa | Jamapa Platy |
| *Xiphophorus maculatus*, San Juan | Gray Platy |
| *Xiphophorus maculatus*, Rio Papaloapan | Black Platy |
| *Xiphophorus maculatus*, Rio Coatzacoalcos marshes | Red Platy |
| *Xiphophorus maculatus*, Belize River | Spotted Belize Platy |
| *Xiphophorus maculatus*, Belize marshes | Red-eyed Platy |
| *Xiphophorus variatus*, Rio Axtla | Parrot Platy |
| *Xiphophorus variatus*, Rio Nautla | Yellow-tailed Platy |
| *Xiphophorus variatus*, Rio Cazone | Cazone Platy |
| *Xiphophorus variatus*, Rio Soto la Marina | Black-banded Platy |
| *Xiphophorus xiphidium*, Rio Purification | Sword Platy |
| *Xiphophorus xiphidium*, Rio Santa Engracia | Black-spotted Sword Platy |

## Varieties

| | |
|---|---|
| *Xiphophorus helleri*, spotted, Belize River | Spotted Belize Swordtail |
| *Xiphophorus helleri*, spotted, Rio Atoyac | Spotted Atoyac Swordtail |
| *Xiphophorus helleri*, red and spotted, Rio Atoyac | Red and spotted Atoyac Swordtail |
| *Xiphophorus pygmaeus*, yellow, Rio Axtla, males only | Yellow Pygmy Swordtail |
| *Xiphophorus nigrensis*, yellow, Rio Coy, males only | Yellow Dwarf Swordtail |
| *Xiphophorus montezumae*, Rio Verde | Black-spotted Montezuma Swordtail |

## Natural Biotope Communities

In the area of occurrence, or range, of the genus *Xiphophorus*, there are numerous bodies of water in which a number of species live together. Hybrids between the species have not yet been observed in the wild. On my (L.W.) *Xiphophorus* collecting expeditions to Mexico in the years 1979, 1980, and 1983, the following *Xiphophorus* communities could be observed:

**Arroyo Chapultepec:** *Xiphophorus kosszanderi* and *Xiphophorus roseni.*

**Rio Atoyac:** *Xiphophorus helleri* in the following populations: unspeckled, speckled, red, as well as red and speckled. *Xiphophorus andersi.*

**Rio Axtla:** *Xiphophorus pygmaeus, Xiphophorus cortezi,* and *Xiphophorus variatus.*

**Rio Nautla:** *Xiphophorus helleri* and *Xiphophorus variatus.*

**Rio dos Semillas:** *Xiphophorus clemenciae* and *Xiphophorus helleri,* population from the Rio Coatzacoalcos system.

**Rio Verde:** *Xiphophorus variatus.*

**Lake Catemaco:** *Xiphophorus helleri,* population from Catemaco, and *Xiphophorus milleri.*

In addition to these, there are also various bodies of water in which *Xiphophorus* species live together with, for example, *Xiphophorus helleri* populations. Populations of *Xiphophorus* species also live in biotope communities. For example, in the Belize River region, *Xiphophorus maculatus* populations live together with *Xiphophorus helleri,* speckled population.

Pool source of the Rio Atoyac biotope of *X. andersi.* Photo by L. Wischnath.

A brook or creek which flows into Rio Nautla. Photo by L. Wischnath.

Rio Nautla, Veracruz, Mexico. Photo by L. Wischnath.

A young male and female *Xiphophorus variatus* from Rio Axtla. Photo by L. Wischnath.

A pair of platies, *Xiphophorus variatus*, from Rio Nautla, Mexico. Photo by L. Wischnath.

Rio dos Semillas, Mexico. Photo by L. Wischnath.

A pair of *Xiphophorus helleri* from Rio dos Semillas. Photo by L. Wischnath.

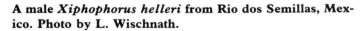

A male *Xiphophorus helleri* from Rio dos Semillas, Mexico. Photo by L. Wischnath.

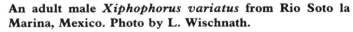

An adult male *Xiphophorus variatus* from Rio Soto la Marina, Mexico. Photo by L. Wischnath.

A pair of brass swordtails, *Xiphophorus helleri,* from Rio del Reyon. Photo by L. Wischnath.

Lake Catemaco, Mexico, home of the brass swordtail. Photo by L. Wischnath.

Rio Palenque, Mexico. Photo by L. Wischnath.

Rio Panuco, Mexico. Photo by L. Wischnath.

*Xiphophorus variatus* male from Rio Cazone, Mexico. Photo by L. Wischnath.

San Andres Tuxtla, Mexico. *Xiphophorus helleri* is collected in these waters. Photo by L. Wischnath.

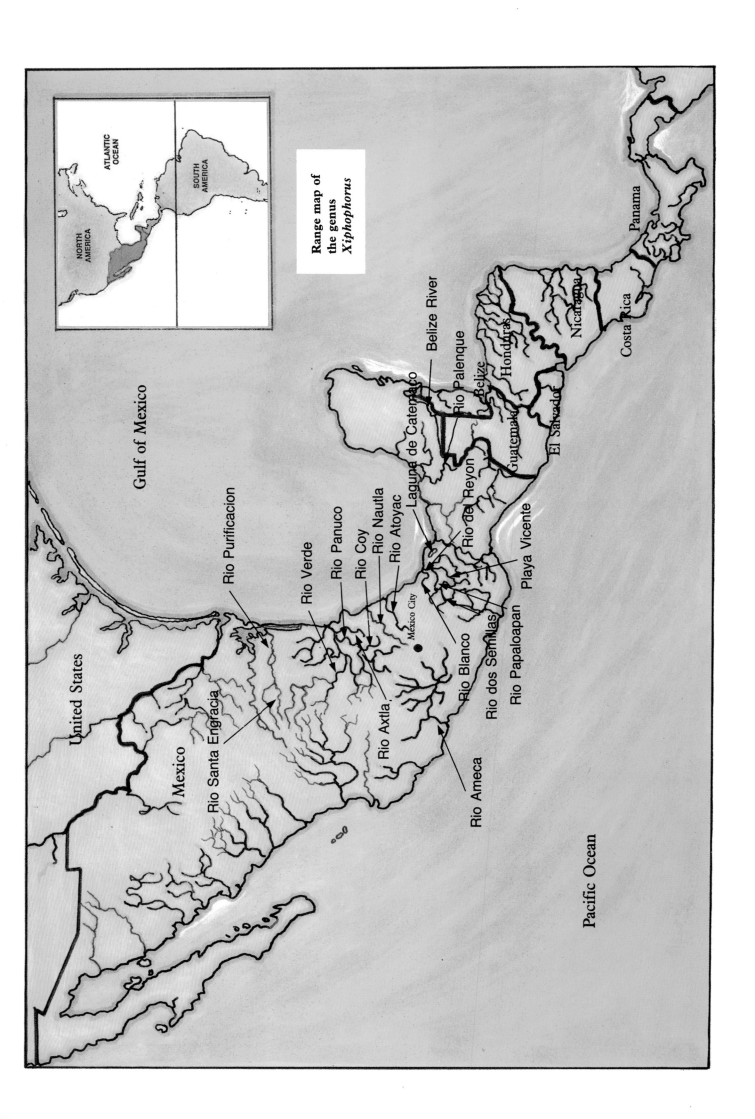

**Range map of the genus *Xiphophorus***

ATLANTIC OCEAN

NORTH AMERICA

SOUTH AMERICA

Gulf of Mexico

United States

Mexico

Rio Santa Engracia

Rio Purificacion

Rio Verde

Rio Panuco

Rio Coy

Rio Nautla

Rio Atoyac

Laguna de Catemaco

Rio Axtla

México City

Rio del Reyon

Rio Blanco

Rio dos Semillas

Rio Papaloapan

Playa Vicente

Rio Ameca

Belize River

Rio Palenque

Belize

Honduras

Guatemala

El Salvador

Nicaragua

Costa Rica

Panama

Pacific Ocean

# *XIPHOPHORUS* WILD FORMS (SWORDTAILS)

## *XIPHOPHORUS PYGMAEUS*
### Hubbs & Gordon, 1943

**Family:** Poeciliidae Garman, 1895.

**Subfamily:** Poeciliinae Garman, 1895.

**Meaning of the specific name:** *pygmaeus* (Latin)—dwarflike; refers to the small body size of the species.

**Synonyms:** *Xiphophorus pygmaeus pygmaeus* Rosen, 1960.

**First description:** Hubbs, C. L. and M. Gordon (1943): Studies of cyprinodont fishes. XIX. *Xiphophorus pygmaeus*, new species from Mexico. *Copeia* (1): pp. 31–33.

**Type locality:** Rio Axtla, San Luis Potosi, Mexico.

*Xiphophorus pygmaeus* **variety with yellow male. Photo by L. Wischnath.**

*Type locality: the specific geographic location where the holotype of a species was collected.*

*Xiphophorus pygmaeus*, **male below. Photo by Dr. C. D. Zander.**

*Xiphophorus pygmaeus* from Rio Axtla. Photo by L. Wischnath.

*"Regular water changes are indispensable for the well-being of these fish."*

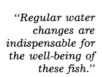

*Meristic data: countable features, such as number of dorsal fin rays (Dorsal), number of scales in a straight series along the side from gill cover to tail base (mLR), and number of vertebrae (Vertebrae).*

**Meristic data:** Dorsal: 9–12 fin rays; mLR: 25–26 scales; vertebrae: 26–27.

**Total body length:** Males up to 3.5 centimeters; females up to 4.5 centimeters.

**Description:** This smallest species of sword-bearing *Xiphophorus* has a gray-brown ground color. Two zigzag lines are present above the brown lateral stripe. The ventral side is white. All fins are transparent. The dorsal fin is adorned with a dark band of commas. In 1980, males with an intense yellow coloration were collected for the first time in the Rio Axtla. It was later proved that no females of this color variety exist. The male's sword is only 1 to 2 millimeters long and is formed from the three lowermost tail-fin rays.

**Range:** Rio Axtla drainage basin, San Luis Potosi, Mexico.

**Habitat:** In the fast-flowing Rio Axtla these swordtails prefer to stay near steep banks. At one collecting site, near the town of Axtla, the river is 30 to 35 meters wide. The average annual water temperature is 22° to 24° C.

**Care and spawning:** This small *Xiphophorus* species is very delicate in captivity. Rarely are more than ten young, 6 to 7 millimeters long, produced by one female. They are generally safe from attacks by the adults. If possible, this species should be given its own tank. Regular water changes are indispensable for the well-being of these fish. Good water movement should be provided by means of return flow from the filter. The diet should consist chiefly of small live food (*Artemia*). The water temperature should be about 24° C.

### *XIPHOPHORUS NIGRENSIS* Rosen, 1960

**Family:** Poeciliidae Garman, 1895.

**Subfamily:** Poeciliinae Garman, 1895.

**Meaning of the specific name:** *nigrensis* (Latin)—with a black sword.

**Synonyms:** *Xiphophorus pygmaeus nigrensis* Rosen, 1960.

**First description:** Rosen, D. E. (1960): "Middle American poeciliid fishes of the genus *Xiphophorus*." *Bull. Florida State Mus., Biol. Sci.*, vol. 5, no. 4: pp. 57–242.

**Type locality:** Rio Choy, San Luis Potosi, Mexico.

**Meristic data:** Dorsal: 11–14 fin rays; mLR: 25–28 scales; vertebrae: 29.

**Total body length:** Males 3 to 6 centimeters; females up to 6 centimeters.

A wild caught pair of *Xiphophorus nigrensis*. Photo by L. Wischnath.

*Synonyms: Taxonomic names of species that are rejected because they were described after the original description of a species and have turned out to be equivalent to that species.*

A pair of normal *X. nigrensis* from San Luis Potosi, Mexico. Photo by L. Wischnath.

The yellow or gold variety of *X. nigrensis*. This color only appears in the male sex. Photo by L. Wischnath.

*Humpbacked: A condition in which the back is more or less angled, often caused by the curvature of the spine; medically known as kyphosis.*

A pair of *Xiphophorus nigrensis*, male above. Photo by Dr. H. R. Axelrod.

**Description:** This species, which is closely related to *Xiphophorus pygmaeus*, occurs in two forms and three color varieties in the male sex. The so-called normal form lives in the Rio Choy. Both sexes attain a length of 5 to 6 centimeters. There is virtually no difference in body coloration between females of *Xiphophorus nigrensis* and those of *Xiphophorus pygmaeus*. *Xiphophorus nigrensis* females are, however, more humpbacked. Males from the Rio Choy have a magnificent sword. The yellow sword can be up to 3 centimeters long and is edged in black only on the underside.

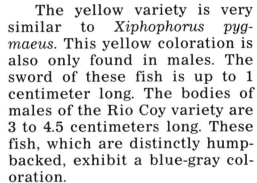

The yellow variety is very similar to *Xiphophorus pygmaeus*. This yellow coloration is also only found in males. The sword of these fish is up to 1 centimeter long. The bodies of males of the Rio Coy variety are 3 to 4.5 centimeters long. These fish, which are distinctly humpbacked, exhibit a blue-gray coloration.

**Range:** Rio Choy and Rio Coy, Rio Panuco basin, San Luis Potosi, Mexico.

**Habitat:** The Rio Choy and the Rio Coy in the Rio Panuco basin are fast flowing and have rapids in some places. The average water temperature is from 23° to 25° C. *Xiphophorus nigrensis* favors steep banks under overhanging riparian vegetation over or in dense stands of aquatic plants.

**Care and spawning:** This species is considered to be the most difficult in the genus *Xiphophorus*. In all *Xiphophorus nigrensis* varieties at most 20 young are produced, which are 6 to 7 millimeters long at birth. Aquarium conditions and feeding are as given for *Xiphophorus pygmaeus*.

## XIPHOPHORUS CORTEZI
## Rosen, 1960

**Family:** Poeciliidae Garman, 1895.

**Subfamily:** Poeciliinae Garman, 1895.

**Meaning of the specific name:** *cortezi*—named after the Spanish conquistador, Hernando Cortez.

**Synonyms:** *Xiphophorus montezumae cortezi* Rosen, 1960.

**First description:** Rosen, D. E. (1960): "Middle American poeciliid fishes of the genus *Xiphophorus*." *Bull. Florida State Mus., Biol. Sci.*, vol. 5, no. 4: pp. 57–242.

**Type locality:** Arroyo Matlapa at Comoca, San Luis Potosi, Mexico.

**Meristic data:** Dorsal: 10–14 fin rays; mLR: 26–28 scales; vertebrae: 28–29.

**Total body length:** Males 4 to 5 centimeters; females 4 to 5.5 centimeters.

**Description:** The Cortez Swordtail has an elongated build. The ground color is gray-brown with a light ventral side. A distinct zigzag line extends horizontally along the middle of the body. Specimens with additional vertical stripes also occur occasionally. A different morph is characterized by a pattern of large black spots. One variety possesses a band of comma-like markings on the base of the tail

A pair of Cortez swordtails, *Xiphophorus cortezi*. Photo by G. J. M. Timmerman.

*Color morph: A member or members of a species that differ in color or pattern from other members of the same species; ex. striped morph versus spotted morph.*

*Xiphophorus cortezi* morph with scattered black spots. Photo by Dr. C. D. Zander.

The male *Xiphophorus cortezi* has a banner-like dorsal fin. Photo by M. Meyer.

*Range: the geographic delimitation of a species.*

*"The spawning of this interesting* Xiphophorus *species presents no problems."*

fin. Males of this species are the only sword-bearing *Xiphophorus* with an up to 2-centimeter-long, upward-curved sword. The male's dorsal fin is banner-like. It is yellow and possesses dark flecks.

**Range:** Upper course of the Rio Panuco, Hidulgo and San Luis Potosi, Mexico.

**Habitat:** As given for *Xiphophorus pygmaeus.*

**Care and spawning:** The spawning of this interesting *Xiphophorus* species presents no problems. The 20 to 40 young produced by the female are about 8 millimeters long. The aquarium should be well planted and should have moving water with a temperature of from 24 to 27° C. Live food must preferentially be given. Vegetable flake food is greatly appreciated. Although no particular demands are made with respect to water quality, partial water changes must be performed regularly.

## XIPHOPHORUS MONTEZUMAE
### Jordan & Snyder, 1900

**Family:** Poeciliidae Garman, 1895.

**Subfamily:** Poeciliinae Garman, 1895.

**Meaning of the specific name:** *montezumae*—named after the Aztec emperor Montezuma II.

**Synonyms:** *Xiphophorus montezumae montezumae* Rosen, 1960.

**First description:** Jordan, D. S. and J. O. Snyder (1900): Notes on a collection of fishes from the rivers of Mexico, with descriptions of twenty new species. *Bull. U.S. Fish Comm.,* for 1899: pp. 115–147.

**Type locality:** Rio Verde, San Luis Potosi, Mexico.

**Meristic data:** Dorsal: 10–14 fin rays; mLR: 25–28 scales; vertebrae: 28–30.

**Total body length:** Males up to 5 centimeters; females up to 6 centimeters.

**Description:** The Montezuma Swordtail has an elongated build. The male's sword is up to 4 centimeters long. It is greenish-yellow and edged in black. In some specimens it may also be an intense pink color. This species' body has four or five brown zigzag lines on a gray ground color. A pattern of bands, consisting of four to seven dark vertical stripes, is present on the body. As a rule, the fins are a yellowish shade. Since 1983, significantly larger specimens have become known. They have a hump-backed form. They can grow to a length of 12 to 14 centimeters. In males, the sword length of 6 to 8 centimeters is added to this. The variety has a gray-brown body coloration.

According to personal communication from Kallman, these specimens represent a native population. A variety from the Rio Verde with an elongated body and a large black spot on the base of the tail is also known. The swords of these males reach a length of from 8 to 10 centimeters.

**Range:** Rio Tamesi drainage, Tamaulipas, and the Rio Salto, San Luis Potosi, Mexico.

**Habitat:** The Rio Salto is fast flowing. Some sites exhibit luxuriant plant growth. The clear water has a temperature of from 24 to 26° C. The same is true of the Rio Verde.

**Care and spawning:** *Xiphophorus montezumae* is not difficult to spawn. The young are 7 to 8 millimeters long at birth. They grow very slowly. Aquarium conditions are as given for *Xiphophorus cortezi.*

*Habitat: the place where a particular species is normally found.*

**Xiphophorus montezumae var. from Rio Verde. Photo by L. Wischnath.**

**X. montezumae or possible hybrid between X. montezumae and X. cortezi.**

**The Montezuma swordtail usually has a well developed sword. Photo courtesy N. Y. Zoological Society.**

*Xiphophorus alvarezi was named in honor of Prof. Jose Alvarez del Villar. Photo by B. Kahl.*

*Family: a taxonomic category based on the grouping of related genera.*

*The range of X. alvarezi includes the upland basin of Chiapas, Mexico, and several localities in Guatemala. Photo by H.-J. Richter.*

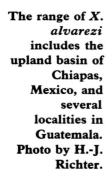

## XIPHOPHORUS ALVAREZI
### Rosen, 1960

**Family:** Poeciliidae Garman, 1895.

**Subfamily:** Poeciliinae Garman, 1895.

**Meaning of the specific name:** *alvarezi*—named in honor of Prof. Jose Alvarez del Villar.

**Synonyms:** *Xiphophorus helleri alvarezi* Rosen, 1960.

**First description:** Rosen, D. E. (1960): "Middle American poeciliid fishes of the genus *Xiphophorus*." *Bull. Florida State Mus., Biol. Sci.*, vol. 5, no. 4: pp. 57–242.

**Type locality:** Rio Santo Domingo, Chiapas, Mexico.

**Meristic data:** Dorsal: 11–12 fin rays; mLR: 26–29 scales; vertebrae: usually 28.

**Total body length:** Males up to 6 centimeters; females up to 7.5 centimeters. Measurements do not include the sword length.

**Description:** In its body dimensions, *Xiphophorus alvarezi* cannot be visually separated from the *Xiphophorus helleri* complex. Discrimination on the basis of sword length is also impossible. Rosen and colleagues

recorded short-sworded specimens in the Rio Candelaria Yalicar, Alta Verapaz, Guatemala. *Xiphophorus alvarezi* possesses two or more red lines along the middle of the body. The color of the sides of the body is intense turquoise blue. The dorsal fin exhibits two rows of bands, which are composed of broad red spots. The male's sword reaches a length of from 4 to 6 centimeters.

**Range:** Upland basin of Chiapas, Mexico and Huehuetenango, El Quiche, and Alta Verapaz, Guatemala.

**Habitat:** Few data on the range are known. In 1980, based on information from the State Aquarium in Tuxtla Gutierrez, Chiapas, Mexico, Wischnath recorded the species near the ruins of Palenque, Chiapas, Mexico. The Rio Palenque is shallow, fast flowing and, in part, torrential.

**Care and spawning:** This species can be designated as undemanding in the aquarium. Nev-

ertheless, it should be kept in aquaria with good water movement and dense plant growth. Regular partial water changes serve the well-being of the fish. The water temperature should be 24 to 27° C. The fish should be fed a varied diet of live, frozen, and dry food. The number of young in a brood is 20 to 40.

## *XIPHOPHORUS CLEMENCIAE* Alvarez, 1959

**Family:** Poeciliidae Garman, 1895.

**Subfamily:** Poeciliinae Garman, 1895.

**Meaning of the specific name:** *clemenciae*—named in honor of Mrs. Clemencia Alvarez.

**Synonyms:** None.

**First description:** Alvarez, J. (1959): Nuevas especies de *Xiphophorus* e *Hyporhamphus* procedents del Rio Coatzacoalcos. *Ciencia*, vol. 19: pp. 69–73.

*First description: citation of the article in which the species was first named.*

**Xiphophorus clemenciae was named in honor of Mrs. Clemencia Alvarez. Photo by L. Wischnath.**

This pair of cultured form of "green" *Xiphophorus helleri,* unlike the wild form of *Xiphophorus clemenciae,* does not have two intense red stripes along the middle of the body. Photo by B. Kahl.

**Type locality:** Rancho San Carlos, 24 kilometers east of Palomares, Oaxaca, Mexico.

**Meristic data:** Dorsal: 9 fin rays; mLR: 25–26 scales; vertebrae: 27.

**Total body length:** Males up to 4 centimeters; females up to 5.5 centimeters.

**Description:** This splendid little species of swordtail has an elongated build. The body ground color is gray-brown to olive. The middle of the body and the caudal peduncle are overlaid with blue. This species, which is threatened with extinction, has two intense red stripes along the middle of the body. The male's lemon-yellow sword, which is edged in black, reaches a length of up to 3.5 centimeters. Typical of the species is the red speckling on the tail fin. All fins have a yellow tinge. The dorsal fin has red spots.

**Range:** Rio Sarabia system, Oaxaca, Mexico.

**Habitat:** J. Alvarez collected the first specimens in 1959 in the Arroyo de la Cascada in the Mexican state of Oaxaca, near Rancho San Carlos, 24 kilometers south of Highways 145 and 185 near the village of Palomares. The Arroyo de la Cascado joins the Rio Sarabia and the Rio Coatzacoalcos west of Palomares. This rare species of fish was reported in the Rio del Reyon and the Rio dos Semillas near Palomares by Wischnath in 1979. Because of flooding, he was not able to establish its presence there in 1983.

**Care and spawning:** This species is very difficult to keep in the aquarium. Tanks with a good flow of water and the best water quality are necessary. The water temperature should be 24° to 26°C. The diet should consist chiefly of live foods (sieved food, *Artemia*). Supplementary vegetable food is important. A female brings about 15 to 20 young into the world at a time. They are very difficult to rear. They generally die after a few weeks because of weakness (vitamin deficiency?). Recently, rearing tanks with heavy growths of algae have proved beneficial.

**Rio dos Semillas, habitat of *X. clemenciae*. Photo by L. Wischnath.**

A pair of *X. signum* from Alta Verapaz, Guatemala. Photo by L. Wischnath.

The name *signum* refers to the comma-shaped mark at the base of the tail. Photo by M. Meyer.

## *XIPHOPHORUS SIGNUM*
### Rosen and Kallman, 1969

**Family:** Poeciliidae Garman, 1895.

**Subfamily:** Poeciliinae Garman, 1895.

**Meaning of the specific name:** *signum* (Latin)—sign; refers to the comma marking on the base of the tail of females.

**Synonyms:** *Xiphophorus helleri signum* Rosen and Kallman, 1969.

**First description:** Rosen, D. E. and K. D. Kallman (1969): A New Fish of the Genus *Xiphophorus* from Guatemala, with Remarks on the Taxonomy of Endemic Forms. *Amer. Mus. Novitates*, no. 2379: pp. 1–29.

**Type locality:** Rio Semococh, Alta Verapaz, Guatemala.

**Meristic data:** Dorsal: 11–13 fin rays; mLR: 28 scales; vertebrae: 29.

**Total body length:** Males up to 7.5 centimeters; females up to 10 centimeters.

**Description:** *Xiphophorus signum* does not differ from *Xiphophorus helleri* in build. Its coloration is gray to olive-brown with a light ventral side. The lateral scale rows gleam in metallic green. The fish generally exhibit a brown horizontal stripe. The male's sword is 3 to 4 centimeters long, seldom longer. It is edged in intense, rich black. The specific name refers to the distinct comma on the female's tail fin.

**Range:** Rio Chajmaic, Rio de la Pasion basin, Alta Verapaz, Guatemala.

**Habitat:** Their habitat has fast-flowing water with steep banks and dense vegetation in the water. The water temperature is between 25° and 27° C.

**Care and spawning:** This species is easy to keep. Tanks should not be too small. A dense planting provides refuges in the fights between the males. Water movement and regular partial water changes are appreciated by the fish. The diet should be varied and should include both live and dry foods. The number of young produced in a brood is 20 to 80.

### *XIPHOPHORUS XIPHIDIUM* (Gordon, 1932)

**Family:** Poeciliidae Garman, 1895.

**Subfamily:** Poeciliinae Garman, 1895.

**Meaning of the specific name:** *xiphidium* (Greek)—small sword-carrier.

**Synonyms:** *Platypoecilus xiphidium* Gordon, 1932. *Xiphophorus variatus xiphidium* Rosen, 1960. *Platypoecilus maculatus* Regan, 1913. *Platypoecilus variatus* Meek, 1904.

**First description:** Gordon, M. (1932): Dr. Myron Gordon going

*Xiphophorus xiphidium* is built like a platy but has a small spike of a sword. Photo courtesy N. Y. Zoological Society.

*Subfamily: a taxonomic category just below the family level that contains a group of genera that can be distinguished from another group of genera within the family.*

A pair of *Xiphophorus xiphidium* from Rio Santa Engracia with the large spot at the tail base. Photo by L. Wischnath.

**A wild caught pair of *X. xiphidium* from Rio Purificacion. Photo by L. Wischnath.**

*"In older males the central body region may be intense blue."*

*Piebald markings: spotted or blotched, usually in black and white.*

on expedition. *Aquatic Life*, vol. 15: pp. 287–288.

**Type locality:** Rio Sota la Marina, Tamaulipas, Mexico.

**Meristic data:** Dorsal: 9–11 fin rays; anal: 9 fin rays; gill rakers: 15–18; mLR: 25–26 scales.

**Total body length:** Males 2.5 centimeters; females up to 4 centimeters.

**Description:** This species has a compact and hump-backed build. The head is small and pointed. The body ground color is olive-brown with a white ventral side. Males develop a small sword. In older males the central body region may be intense blue. Occasionally, specimens with piebald markings also occur. The fins are usually transparent, although they may also

*X. "kosszanderi„ is a natural hybrid between X. variatus and X. xiphidium. It occurs at Rio Soto la Marina. Photo by L. Wischnath.*

*"Xiphophorus xiphidium . . . favors shallow and muddy bodies of water."*

*Tributary: a stream feeding a larger stream, river or lake.*

have a yellow tinge. A population from the Rio Santa Engracia, a tributary of the Rio Purificacion, which differs clearly from the previously known populations, has been known since 1979. This population has a prominent yellow-bordered black spot in the area of the base of the tail.

**Range:** Rio Sota la Marina system, Tamaulipas, Mexico. Favors shallow and muddy bodies of water. Ponds and irrigation ditches are also inhabited.

**Care and spawning:** This species is an undemanding charge in the aquarium. Failures are rare. Plants and a temperature of 26° to 28° C are appreciated. The female produces 15 to 30 young, occasionally more. The fish should be offered a varied diet.

A pair of *X. andersi* from Veracruz, Mexico. Photo by L. Wischnath.

The small sword of this *X. andersi* is highlighted against the plant leaf in this photo by L. Wischnath.

The Rio Atoyac, Veracruz, Mexico. Photo by L. Wischnath.

## *XIPHOPHORUS ANDERSI* Meyer and Schartl, 1980

**Family:** Poeciliidae Garman, 1895.

**Subfamily:** Poeciliinae Garman, 1895.

**Meaning of the specific name:** *andersi*—named in honor of Prof. F. Anders.

**Synonyms:** None.

**First description:** Meyer, M. K. and M. Schartl (1980): Eine neue *Xiphophorus*-Art aus Vera Cruz, Mexico. *Senckenbergiana Biologica* 60 (3–4): pp. 147–151.

**Type locality:** Rio Atoyac, near Chico, Veracruz, Mexico.

**Meristic data:** Dorsal: 12 fin rays; anal: 10 fin rays; Ltr: 9 scales; mLR: 27–28 scales; vertebrae: 29.

**Total body length:** Males up to 4.5 centimeters; females up to 5.5 centimeters.

**Description:** This *Xiphophorus* species has a large head. The moderately slender body has an elongated caudal peduncle. The dorsal fin is distinctly rhomboid. Three ventral rays of the tail fin are elongated into a short sword. The ground color of both sexes is brown to olive. A brown central stripe extends along the middle of the body. Both sexes exhibit a so-called gravid spot above the anal pore.

**Range:** Known only from the type locality.

**Habitat:** The Rio Atoyac is a fast-flowing river. At the collecting site it is about 6 meters wide and about 2 meters deep. In its small range, *Xiphophorus andersi* lives together with *Xiphophorus helleri*.

**Care and spawning:** Hardly any problems turn up in aquarium keeping. Well-planted tanks with water movement ensure the well-being of the fish. Soft water (8° dH) is preferred. Females produce 20 to 50 about six-millimeter-long young per brood. If they are offered a good diet of live and dry foods, the adults do not prey on the young. Bloodworms are particularly prized.

## *XIPHOPHORUS HELLERI*
### Heckel, 1848

**Family:** Poeciliidae Garman, 1895.

**Subfamily:** Poeciliinae Garman, 1895.

**Meaning of the specific name:** *helleri*—named after the collector, Carl Heller.

**Synonyms:** *Xiphophorus helleri helleri* Del Campo, 1938. *Xiphophorus guentheri* Jordan and Everman, 1896. *Xiphophorus hel-leri guentheri* Hubbs, 1935. *Xiphophorus jalapae* Meek, 1902. *Xiphophorus strigatus* Regan, 1907. *Xiphophorus helleri strigatus* De Buen, 1940. *Xiphophorus brevis* Regan, 1907. *Xiphophorus helleri brevis* Hubbs and Gordon, 1943. *Xiphophorus rachovi* Regan, 1911.

**First description:** Heckel, J. (1848): Eine neue Gattung von Poecilien mit rochenartigem Anklammerungsorgan. *Sitzber. K. Akad. Wiss. Wien, Math. Nat. Cl.*, vol. 1: pp. 289–303.

**Type locality:** Orizaba, Mexico.

**Meristic data:** Dorsal: usually 12 to 15 fin rays; mLR: usually 26 to 28 scales; vertebrae: 27–30.

**Total body length:** Males up to 14 centimeters; females up to 16 centimeters. This is added to a sword length of 4 to 8 centimeters in the male.

**Description:** *Xiphophorus helleri* has an elongated build. Numerous color morphs live in the very large range. Probably the

*Soft water: water low in calcium and magnesium salts, usually defined as less than 10°dH.*

*"Numerous color morphs live in the very large range."*

**A wild caught pair of *X. helleri* from Rio Nautla, Mexico. Photo by L. Wischnath.**

**A section of the Rio Nautla, Veracruz, Mexico. Photo by L. Wischnath.**

*Ventral: bottom or lower part of a fish as compared with the dorsal or top (back) of the fish and the lateral or side of the fish.*

**A spotted variety of X. helleri from Rio Nautla, Mexico. Note the short sword. Photo by L. Wischnath.**

most familiar of these is the so-called Green Swordtail.

All *Xiphophorus helleri* populations and varieties share the dark-red or brown central stripe. In some regional forms, up to four additional body stripes, two above and two below the central stripe, may be present. The ventral side gener-ally is white and the dorsal fin exhibits red dots of variable intensity. The male's sword is edged in rich yellow and black. Black-speckled specimens have been found in many *Xiphophorus helleri* biotopes. Isolated specimens with vertical stripes also occur.

In November of 1979, Wischnath for the first time established the existence of red and speckled as well as red, unspeckled fish in the Rio Playa Vicente and in the Rio Atoyac, both in the Mexican state of Veracruz.

**Range:** From the Rio Nautla, Veracruz, Mexico as far as Belize and Honduras in lowlands and uplands.

**Habitat:** This species chiefly inhabits fast-flowing streams and rivers, but also occurs in flooded areas, ponds, and lakes. It does not require a uniform

habitat and is found everywhere within its range.

**Care and spawning:** This species is very easy to keep and spawn. Large tanks should, however, be used. Water movement is beneficial, as are a dense planting and sufficient swimming space. The water temperature should be 22° to 28° C. The diet should consist of fortifying foods, both live and dry. Depending on the population, a female brings 40 to 80 young into the world at a time, sometimes more.

Rio Blanco, Veracruz, Mexico, home of *Xiphophorus helleri*. Photo by L. Wischnath.

*Xiphophorus helleri* habitat at the Rio del Reyon, Mexico. Photo by L. Wischnath.

The Lake Catemaco flood zone where *Xiphophorus helleri* can be collected. Photo by L. Wischnath.

Collecting area at Rio del Reyon, Mexico. Photo by L. Wischnath.

*X. helleri* being collected at Rio Playa Vicente, Mexico. Photo by L. Wischnath.

*Xiphophorus helleri*, albino male.

*Xiphophorus helleri*, female.

*Xiphophorus helleri*, spotted male.

*Xiphophorus helleri*, spotted female.

*Xiphophorus helleri*, Rio Blanco male.

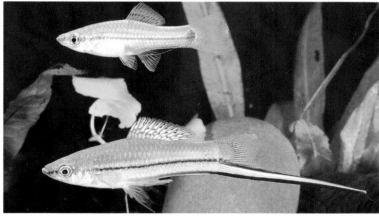

*Xiphophorus helleri*, Rio Atoyac pair.

*Xiphophorus helleri*, Catemaco male.

*Xiphophorus helleri*, hobby strain male.

*Xiphophorus cortezi*, male.

*Xiphophorus cortezi*, male.

*Xiphophorus cortezi*, pair.

*Xiphophorus montezumae*, Tamasopo male.

*Xiphophorus montezumae*, male.

*Xiphophorus montezumae*, female.

*Xiphophorus montezumae*, male.

*Xiphophorus montezumae*, male.

*Xiphophorus milleri*, pair.　　　　　　*Xiphophorus milleri*, pair.

*Xiphophorus cortezi*, blue variation male.　　　*Xiphophorus cortezi*, blue variation female.

*Xiphophorus cortezi*, blue variation male.　　　*Xiphophorus cortezi*, blue variation female.

*Xiphophorus cortezi*, spotted male.　　　　*Xiphophorus montezumae*, male.

*Xiphophorus nigrensis*, male.    *Xiphophorus nigrensis*, female.

*Xiphophorus nigrensis*, male.    *Xiphophorus nigrensis*, pair, short-sword variety.

*Xiphophorus pygmaeus*, male.    *Xiphophorus pygmaeus*, female.

*Xiphophorus signum*, male.    *Xiphophorus signum*, female.

*Xiphophorus clemenciae*, male. *Xiphophorus clemenciae*, female.

*Xiphophorus variatus*, pair. *Xiphophorus couchianus*, Apodaca population pair.

*Xiphophorus evelynae*, Necaxa population male. *Xiphophorus evelynae*, Necaxa population female.

*Xiphophorus gordoni*, male. *Xiphophorus gordoni*, male.

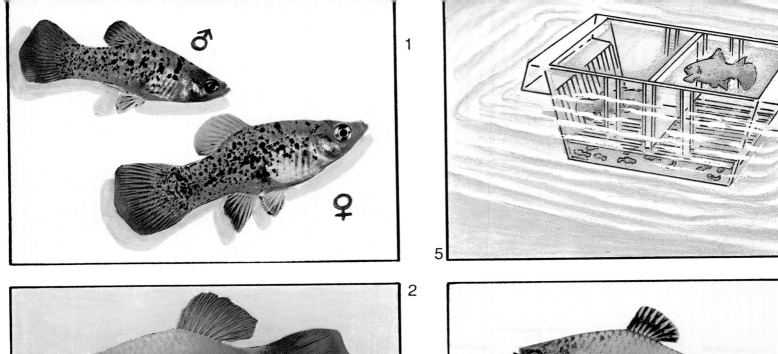

1

5

2

6

3

7

4

8

*Above:* **A pair of gold complete moon platies,** *Xiphophorus maculatus,* **with "Mickey Mouse" design. Photo by H.-J. Richter.**

*Opposite:* **1. Male (above) and female (below) platy. 2. Details of male's gonopodium. 3. Well planted tank for platy breeding. 4. Fertilization of female by male. 5. Females dropping young in breeding trap. 6. Female platy giving birth to living young. 7. Male parent feeding on young. 8. Different varieties of the common platy. Illustrations by John R. Quinn.**

*Xiphophorus xiphidium* male, Rio Purificacion population.

*Xiphophorus xiphidium* male, Santa Engracia population.

*Xiphophorus couchianus* male, Apodaca population.

*Xiphophorus couchianus* female, Apodaca population.

*Xiphophorus milleri* pair, Lake Catemaco.

*Xiphophorus variatus* male, Rio Axtla population.

*Xiphophorus evelynae* male, Necaxa population.

*Xiphophorus evelynae* female, Necaxa population.

# *XIPHOPHORUS* WILD FORMS (PLATIES)

## *XIPHOPHORUS COUCHIANUS* (Girard, 1859)

**Family:** Poeciliidae Garman, 1895.

**Subfamily:** Poeciliinae Garman, 1895.

**Meaning of the specific name:** *couchianus*—named after D. N. Couch.

**Synonym:** *Limia couchiana* Girard, 1859.

**First description:** Girard, C. (1859). Ichthyological notices, 41–59. *Proc. Acad. Nat. Sci. Philadelphia*, no. 11: pp. 113–122.

**Type locality:** Monterrey, Nuevo Leon, Mexico.

**Meristic data:** Dorsal: 9 fin rays; anal: 9 fin rays; gill rakers: 13–17; L. lat.:25–27 scales.

**Total body length:** Males 2 to 2.5 centimeters, females 3 to 4 centimeters.

**Description:** The *Xiphophorus couchianus* form that was described from Huasteca Canyon near Monterrey is already extinct in its natural habitat. The species exhibits an elongated build. In contrast to males, females have a deep, plump form. The dorsal fin is similar in form to that of *Xiphophorus variatus*, but is considerably smaller in size. The dorsal fin is a light yellow color in Alpha males and its rays are black in both sexes. All remaining fins are colorless. The ground color of this swordless *Xiphophorus* is not especially attractive and is made up of variable shades of brown. The ventral side is white; a dark spot is present in front of the anal fin. Depending on stimulation, three to five broad, dark vertical stripes may be displayed along the sides of the body.

*Alpha male: strongest or most dominant male in a breeding group; this male is usually the most colorful when compared to subordinate individuals.*

*"The Xiphophorus couchianus form that was described from Huasteca Canyon near Monterrey is already extinct in its natural habitat."*

**Wild pair of *Xiphophorus couchianus*. Photo by L. Wischnath.**

*Extinction: worldwide death and disappearance of a specific organism or group of organisms.*

*"Today, only the Apodaca form . . . still exists in the wild in a very limited biotope."*

**Range:** Up to the year 1964, this species occurred in and around Monterrey in headwaters, rivers, and ponds. Today only the Apodaca form, which may be a subspecies of *Xiphophorus couchianus*, still exists in the wild in a very limited biotope.

**Habitat:** At one time Monterrey possessed a fairly large number of headwaters of rivers, which today have partially dried up or only flow periodically. At that time La Huasteca was a residual body of water, which has completely dried up today. Ponds are polluted and in those places where *couchianus* still exists it has been displaced by introduced fishes or has hybridized with *Xiphophorus variatus* and *Xiphophorus* strains.

**Care and spawning:** The spawning of *Xiphophorus couchianus*, Huasteca form, frequently presents problems, since the males cannot always fertilize the females. This *Xiphophorus* species prefers soft water with a temperature of 20° to 23° C. After a gestation period that averages 28 days, between 15 and 30 about 5-millimeter-long fry are produced, which are often born with an enlarged yolk sac.

*Xiphophorus couchianus* generally becomes sexually mature after 10 to 12 weeks. This *Xiphophorus* species is satisfied with small aquaria and makes no demands with respect to diet. Feeding with *Artemia* seems to be beneficial to the well-being of the fish. With infestations of external parasites, 60 drops of 4% formalin per gallon of water has proven to be a particularly effective remedy.

### *Xiphophorus couchianus* "apodaca"

### (Apodaca population, Nuevo Leon, Mexico).

This type possibly represents a new *couchianus* form; its coloration is much different than that of the Huasteca variety, which has already become extinct in the wild. Morphological differences between the different *couchianus* forms have not yet been clearly defined. The so-called Apodaca form is the last strain of *Xiphophorus couchianus* still living in the wild. The population size is estimated to be about 1000.

**Xiphophorus "roseni," a natural hybrid between X. couchianus and X. variatus. Photo by L. Wischnath.**

*Xiphophorus evelynae* was named in honor of Evelyn Gordon. Photo by L. Wischnath.

## XIPHOPHORUS EVELYNAE
### Rosen, 1960

**Family:** Poeciliidae Garman, 1895.

**Subfamily:** Poeciliinae Garman, 1895.

**Meaning of the specific name:** *evelynae*—named in honor of Mrs. Evelyn Gordon, Dr. Myron Gordon's wife.

**Synonym:** *Xiphophorus variatus evelynae* Rosen, 1960.

**First description:** Rosen, D. E. (1960): Middle-American poeciliid fishes of the genus *Xiphophorus. Bull. Florida State Mus., Biol. Sci.,* vol. 5, no. 4: pp. 57–242.

**Type locality:** Rio Necaxa, Puebla, Mexico.

**Meristic data:** Dorsal: 11–14 fin rays; L. lat.:24–27 scales; vertebrae: 27–28.

**Total body length:** Males up to 4.5 centimeters, females up to 5 centimeters.

**Description:** *Xiphophorus evelynae* is closely related to *Xiphophorus variatus* and is virtually identical in external appearance with the former nominate form. In comparison, *evelynae* exhibits an elongated build and a constant coloration, which differs from that of *variatus*. The caudal peduncle of *Xiphophorus evelynae* is short. Six to ten dark vertical stripes extend along the sides of the body. Markings on the caudal peduncle, such as are found in *Xiphophorus variatus* and *Xiphophorus maculatus*, are completely absent in *Xiphophorus evelynae*. Males and females are usually speckled with black.

Specimens without visible spots are occasionally found. The ground color of the body is olive brown with a light ventral side. The fins of males, particularly the dorsal and caudal fins,

"Xiphophorus evelynae *is closely related to* Xiphophorus variatus *and is virtually identical in external appearance with the former nominate form.*"

Caudal peduncle: the part of a fish at the base of the tail, usually measured from the end of the anal or dorsal fin to the base of the caudal fin.

The biotope of *Xiphophorus gordoni*, Coahuila, Mexico. Photo by L. Wischnath.

may be deep yellow to orange colored. In females the fins have either a light yellow tint or are transparent.

**Range:** Rio Tecolutla system, Puebla, Mexico.

**Habitat:** *Xiphophorus evelynae* is collected above a series of waterfalls, in and in the immediate vicinity of the small village of Necaxa, Puebla, Mexico. This livebearer chiefly occurs in reservoirs and the streams flowing into them owned by the Mexican Power and Light Authority, at an estimated elevation of 1,220 meters above sea level. Close to where *Xiphophorus evelynae* occurs, so-called intermediate forms between *evelynae* and *variatus* are also found, which at the moment are classified with *Xiphophorus variatus*.

# *XIPHOPHORUS GORDONI*
## Miller and Minckley, 1963

**Family:** Poeciliidae Garman, 1895.

**Subfamily:** Poeciliinae Garman, 1895.

**Meaning of the specific name:** *gordoni*—named in honor of Dr. Myron Gordon.

**Synonyms:** None.

**First description:** Miller, R. R. and W. L. Minckley (1963): *Xiphophorus gordoni*, a New Species of Platyfish from Coahuila, Mexico. *Copeia*, No. 3: pp. 538–546.

**Type locality:** Laguna Santa Tecla, Coahuila, Mexico.

*Platy: member of the genus Xiphophorus without a visible prolongation of the lower edge of the caudal fin, i.e., no sword.*

**Xiphophorus gordoni, male. Photo by L. Wischnath.**

**Care and spawning:** This species must be kept at somewhat cooler temperatures. Water temperatures of between 20° and 22° C are more than adequate and are necessary for the well-being of the fish. *Xiphophorus evelynae* is more difficult to spawn than *Xiphophorus variatus*, but can still be described as easy to spawn. Otherwise, as in *Xiphophorus variatus*.

*Gill rakers: bony processes located on the inner edge of the gill arches that prevent the passage of solid substances through the gill clefts.*

*Pathogen: a disease-producing organism.*

*"This species, which is threatened with extinction, is particularly susceptible to pathogens . . ."*

**Meristic data:** Dorsal: usually 11 fin rays; anal: 9 fin rays; gill rakers: 15–19; L. lat.:26–27 scales.

**Total body length:** Males 2.5 to 3.5 centimeters, females 3 to 4 centimeters.

**Description:** *Xiphophorus gordoni* possess a moderately elongated build and a pointed head. The ground color of the body is gray-brown with a light ventral side. A blue and black band in the usual *Xiphophorus* zigzag pattern extends along the median scale rows. A black banding on the body, consisting of five to seven broad, vertical stripes, is generally visible only in males. The dorsal fin of males is edged in black. All of the fin rays of the dorsal are black and the fin membranes are a light-yellow.

**Range:** Known only from the type locality.

**Habitat:** According to the findings of Erich Hnilicka, Puebla, Mexico, *Xiphophorus gordoni* lives in source ponds and streams in the region of Santa Tecla at a temperature of 34° C. The small biotope is overgrown with reeds and the streams have dense growths of aquatic plants. The substrate of these waters is muddy and has a strong smell of sulphides.

**Care and spawning:** This species, which is threatened with extinction, is particularly susceptible to pathogens, and for this reason should be offered a water temperature of at least 28° C. *Xiphophorus gordoni* eats its young. Therefore, precautionary measures, such as dense plantings or breeding traps, should be provided. Otherwise, see *Xiphophorus couchianus.*

## *XIPHOPHORUS MILLERI* Rosen, 1960

**Family:** Poeciliidae Garman, 1895.

**Subfamily:** Poeciliinae Garman, 1895.

**Meaning of the specific name:** *milleri*—named in honor of Dr. Robert Rush Miller.

**Synonyms:** None.

**First description:** Rosen, D. E. (1960): Middle-American poeciliid fishes of the genus *Xiphophorus. Bull. Florida State Mus., Biol. Sci.,* vol. 5, no. 4: pp. 57–242.

**Type locality:** Catemaco, Veracruz, Mexico.

**Meristic data:** Dorsal: 9–11 fin rays; L. lat.:25–27 scales; vertebrae: 28.

**Total body length:** Males up to 2.5 cm, females up to 4.5 millimeters.

**Description:** *Xiphophorus milleri* is a small fish in comparison to other representatives of the genus. The males are elongated, while the females, because of their more humpbacked build, look more compact. Both sexes are gray-brown with a light ventral side. A large percentage of the fish possess a small, round black spot at the base of the tail. Adult males also exhibit a fine, black body striping made up of several longitudinal stripes that extend from the front of the body into the caudal peduncle.

Miller reports that fully grown males are supposed to have a deep-orange coloration on the ventral side. Unfortunately, the expected orange tint has not yet been observed among numerous tank-bred fish. H. Stefan, Vienna, is the only one so far who has been able to

Two males and a female *Xiphophorus milleri*. Photo by L. Wischnath.

"*Xiphophorus milleri principally occurs in shallow streams flowing into Lake Catemaco.*"

*Gonopodium: a copulatory organ formed from the modified anal fin.*

**Biotope of *Xiphophorus milleri*.**

see this color pattern in a few fish in the aquarium. Based on Miller's findings, no orange-colored males have been found in the wild. A few males with a black-colored gonopodium are occasionally found.

**Range:** Known only from the type locality.

**Habitat:** *Xiphophorus milleri* principally occurs in shallow streams flowing into Lake Catemaco. It lives there sympatrically with a *Xiphophorus helleri* population from Catemaco, as well as with *Heterandria bimaculata*.

Lake Catemaco, located in the Mexican State of Veracruz, is about 25 kilometers long and 20 kilometers wide. The largest town on the lake is the small town of Catemaco. The vegetation in the vicinity of Lake Catemaco consists of forest, scrub-land, and fields. The bodies of water that enter the lake have a width of 2 to 10 meters and a depth of 20 to 200 centimeters (normal water levels). Luxuriant plant growth is found only sporadically. *Xiphophorus milleri* is found there in large numbers

and often occurs in schools. The fish are not found in large numbers in the lake itself. They chiefly occur in shallow riparian areas at depths of up to 10 centimeters.

*Riparian: living or located at a river bank.*

**Care and spawning:** The breeding of *Xiphophorus milleri* in most cases presents difficulties because maturing fish, above all males, do not attain the size of wild fish. Males are already sexually mature after about three months at a length of one centimeter. Whereas females continue to grow to a length of about three centimeters, males stop growing at a length of between one and one-and-a-half centimeters. In a well-bred stock, females regularly produce between 15 and 50 about 5-millimeter-long fry every 24 to 28 days. Only rarely do adults eat the fry. Although it prefers *Artemia, Xiphophorus milleri* can be described as a fish that eats all kinds of food. The species can be kept in small aquaria with a capacity of 40 liters. The preferred water temperature is 26° C.

*"Males are sexually mature after three months at a length of one centimeter."*

# XIPHOPHORUS MACULATUS (Günther, 1866)

**Family:** Poeciliidae Garman, 1895.

**Subfamily:** Poeciliinae Garman, 1895.

**Meaning of the specific name:** *maculatus* (Latin)—speckled.

**Synonyms:** *Platypoecilus maculatus* Günther, 1866. *Poecilia maculata* Regan, 1906.

**First description:** Günther, A. (1866): *A catalogue of the fishes in the British Museum.* London, vol. 6: 368 pp.

**Type locality:** Mexico, not further defined.

**Meristic data:** Dorsal: usually 9–10 fin rays; L. lat.:22–25 scales; vertebrae: 26–27.

**Total body length:** Males up to 3 centimeters, females up to 4 centimeters.

**Description:** This species exhibits a compact, hump-backed form. *Xiphophorus variatus* is very variable in coloration. Males are generally more in-

*Xiphophorus maculatus* **from the Belize River. Photo by L. Wischnath.**

A pair (male above) of aquarium-bred *Xiphophorus maculatus*. The blue coloring of these fish is especially pronounced. Photo by Dr. Herbert R. Axelrod.

*Xiphophorus maculatus* **male, Rio Papaloapan.**

*Xiphophorus maculatus* **female, Rio Jamapa.**

*Xiphophorus maculatus* **male, Belize.**

*Xiphophorus variatus* **male, Rio Mante.**

tensely marked than females. Lacquer-black males with a light ventral side were observed in the headwaters of the Arroyo Zacatispan, in the Rio Papaloapan region. Orange- and red-marked populations are mostly collected in Belize. In recent years, black-spotted fish have been discovered virtually thoughout the natural areas of distribution. The fins are also very variable in coloration.

**Range:** From the Rio Jamapa basin, Veracruz, Mexico, south to Belize and Guatemala.

**Habitat:** The marshy landscape around Villahermosa, Mexico, is known to be a fairly large habitat of *Xiphophorus maculatus*. The numerous ponds that are found there, which are fed with groundwater, are sometimes connected with rivers in the rainy season. The ponds have dense growths of water hyacinth and the substrate is peaty, so that it is difficult to collect fish there. In various places *maculatus* can be found together with *Xiphophorus helleri*, usually in residual pools. *Xiphophorus maculatus* apparently avoids fast-flowing rivers and is therefore usually encountered only in almost standing bodies of water.

**Care and spawning:** As a rule, *Xiphophorus maculatus* spawns readily and makes no great demands with respect to diet and water quality. Populations with an unstable sex character, in which males are only rarely able to fertilize females, are kept now and then. Certain morphs from the Belize River, for example *Xiphophorus maculatus* (red iris), are particularly susceptible to disease. After a gestation period that averages 24 days, the female produces between 20 and 80 about five-millimeter-long fry. *Xiphophorus maculatus* only rarely eats its young. The species should be kept at a temperature of at least 28° C. Small tanks suffice for successful keeping.

*Xiphophorus maculatus* male, Rio Jamapa.

**Xiphophorus maculatus pair from Rio Papaloapan. Photo by L. Wischnath.**

*Xiphophorus maculatus* male, Belize River.

*Xiphophorus variatus* female, Rio Mante.

*Xiphophorus maculatus* pair from the Belize River, Belize. Photo by L. Wischnath.

*Xiphophorus maculatus* from the Belize River, Belize. Photo by L. Wischnath.

*Xiphophorus maculatus* from Rio Coatzacoalcos. Photo by L. Wischnath.

Rio Jamapa pair of *Xiphophorus maculatus*. Photo by L. Wischnath.

Rio Papaloapan biotope where *Xiphophorus maculatus* is collected. Photo by L. Wischnath.

*Xiphophorus maculatus* male.

*Xiphophorus variatus* female.

*Xiphophorus maculatus* male.

*Xiphophorus maculatus* female.

*Xiphophorus maculatus* male.

*Xiphophorus maculatus* male.

*Xiphophorus maculatus* male.

*Xiphophorus maculatus* female.

*Tail pattern: variable markings on the caudal peduncle at the base of the tail fin.*

# XIPHOPHORUS VARIATUS
## (Meek, 1904)

**Family:** Poeciliidae Garman, 1895.

**Subfamily:** Poeciliinae Garman, 1895.

**Meaning of the specific name:** *variatus* (Latin)—variable, referring to the variable body coloration of male fish.

**Synonyms:** *Platypoecilus variatus* Meek, 1904.

**First description:** Meek, S. E. (1904): The fresh water fishes from Mexico north of the Isthmus of Tehuantepec. *Field Columbian Mus. Publ., zool. ser.,* vol. 5: pp. 1–252.

**Type locality:** Cd. Valles, San Luis Potosi, Mexico.

**Meristic data:** Dorsal: 9–14 fin rays; L. lat.:25–28 scales; vertebrae: 28–30.

**Total body length:** Males up to 4.5 centimeters, females up to 5.5 centimeters.

**Description:** As can be seen from the specific name, this live-bearing toothcarp exhibits a variable body coloration. Almost every conceivable color variety occurs in the wild. Common to almost all *Xiphophorus variatus* males are vertical stripes on the sides of the body as well as variable markings on the caudal peduncle, which are called the tail pattern. These

**A wild pair of *Xiphophorus variatus* from Rio Axtla. Photo by L. Wischnath.**

tail patterns include the one spot, twin spot, Guatemala crescent, simple crescent, and complete moon. All of these markings of the caudal peduncle also occur in *Xiphophorus maculatus*. The tail pattern is usually found in both sexes. Females exhibit a gray-brown body coloration with one or more fine, central stripes. Wild males can be blue, yellow, brown, violet, gray, or orange. Black-spotted fish also occur frequently. The fins are usually transparent or have a yellowish tinge. Fish with an intense orange-colored tail fin are collected in the Rio Axtla. The fry are usually gray brown.

**Range:** From the Rio Soto La Marina system, Tamaulipas, as far as the Rio Nautla, Veracruz, Mexico.

**Habitat:** *Xiphophorus variatus* usually inhabits the shallow riparian regions of slow-flowing or standing bodies of water. This *Xiphophorus* species also occurs in ponds bordering rivers. In some places this toothcarp lives regionally with *Xiphophorus helleri* or *Xiphophorus pygmaeus*, *Xiphophorus cortezi*, *Xiphophorus montezumae*, *Flexipenis vittatus*, *Poecilia sphenops*, *Gambusia atrora*, *Heterandria jonesi*, *Poecilia mexicana*, cichlids, as well as other fishes. In some areas *Xiphophorus variatus* also inhabits fairly cold rivers at water

A wild pair of *Xiphophorus variatus* from Rio Nautla, Mexico. Photo by L. Wischnath.

*Xiphophorus variatus* male.

*Xiphophorus variatus* female.

*Xiphophorus variatus* male.

*Xiphophorus variatus* male, Rio Nautla.

*Xiphophorus variatus* male, Rio Axtla.

*Xiphophorus variatus* female, Rio Axtla.

*X. xiphidium* male, Rio Santa Engracia.

*Xiphophorus xiphidium* male, Rio Purificacion.

temperatures as low as 17° C. For further information on habitat, see *Xiphophorus pygmaeus*.

**Care and spawning:** This species is a very productive spawner. Depending on the size of the female, up to 100 young can be produced. In comparison with other poeciliids, these fish grow very slowly, but can, however, be sexually mature after the fourth month of life. Males become fully colored late and not infrequently do not display their full splendor until they are two years old.

### *Xiphophorus* spec., Muzquiz Platy *

A new *Xiphophorus* species was discovered in 1982 by Dr. Salvador Contreras Balderas from the University of Monterrey, in the Muzquiz headwaters in the Mexican State of Coahuila. Contreras is supposed to provide a scientific name. This *Xiphophorus* species has a pointed head and a moderately elongated build. The ground color of the body is brown. The ventral side is white. An intense black speckling is found along the sides of the body. In places it is composed of so-called T-melanophores. Fish marked with blue also occur. Both sexes are about the same color, and they possess a relatively large gravid spot. Males reach a total length of about 4 centimeters and females a length of 5 centimeters. In build, the Muzquiz

* The Musquiz platy recently has been formally described as *Xiphophorus meyeri* Schartl and Shroeder, 1988. Shortly after this description appeared, a second description by Obregon and Contreras (1988) appeared with the name *X. marmoratus* for the same fish. This latter name becomes a synonym of *X. meyeri*. (Schartl & Shoreder, *Senckenb. Biol.*, 68(4/6): 311-321).

Platy calls to mind *Xiphophorus couchianus*. The Mexican scientist made the following observations on the type locality:

The fish prefer to stay in two albercas (ponds), which serve the native population as natural places for bathing. These water basins are fed by warm-water springs. The crystal-clear water is conducted from mines. A small stream flows from the reservoirs in the direction of the village of Muzquiz. On September 22, 1982, a water temperature of 25° C was measured. The substrate of the home waters consists chiefly of mud. Luxuriant plant growth is found in some places. The platies prefer to stay among the plants.

In the meantime, these fish have made their way into the tanks of fanciers of the wild forms of livebearers. They prove to be demanding charges. The water temperature should be maintained at 25 to 27° C. Water movement must be provided by means of a powerful filter. At temperatures below or above the mentioned values, as well as in stagnant aquarium water, the Muzquiz Platies exhibit discom-

**Collecting site at the Rio Nautla. Photo by L. Wischnath.**

77

*Ichthyologist: a scientist that specializes in the study of fishes.*

**Musquiz platies, *Xiphophorus meyeri,* are not easy to raise. Large aquaria with good water movement are needed. Photo by L. Wischnath.**

fort. These active swimmers need fairly large aquaria. Corresponding to their need for movement, the tank should be planted only in the back and along the sides in order to provide ample swimming space. Females give birth to 15 to 35 young approximately every 28 days. The offspring prefer to hide on the bottom in their first days of life. Later they move to the water's surface. They should be fed with *Artemia.*

The main food for adults should consist of live or frozen foods. Occasional supplements of vegetable dry food are readily taken, but don't use Tetramin flakes.

## Natural *Xiphophorus* hybrids

The ichthyologist Dr. Donn Eric Rosen first reported on natural hybrids of the genus *Xiphophorus* in 1979. He wrote about a *Xiphophorus alvarezi/Xiphophorus helleri* from the Rio Usimacinta system in Guatemala. In 1980, two platies that were unknown up till then were brought to a scientific institute for the first time through the efforts of L. Wischnath, Berlin. On the occasion of an expedition to Mexico, the fish were collected in the Rio Purificacion and in the Arroyo Chapultepec, near the town of Monterrey. All indications were that it was a question of two new *Xiphophorus* species. With the support of the Genetic Institute of the University of Giessen, in 1981 they were described scientifically as *Xiphophorus roseni* Meyer and Wischnath, 1981 (yellow platy) and *Xiphophorus kosszanderi* Meyer and Wischnath, 1981 (spotted platy). They were named in honor of Dr. Rosen and Professors Kosserig and Zander.

Two years later, after intensive observation in aquaria, it turned out that the fishes varied significantly in form and coloration after several generations, so that their status as independent species can no longer be supported. It was determined that it was a question of natural hybrids. *Xiphophorus roseni* is clearly a hybrid of *Xiphophorus couchianus* and *Xiphophorus variatus,* whereas *Xiphophorus kosszanderi* is a hybrid of *Xiphophorus xiphidium* and *Xiphophorus variatus.* It was not clear whether the remnant population of *Xiphophorus couchianus* interbred with wild populations of *Xiphophorus variatus* (northeastern limit of the range of *Xiphophorus variatus*), or if strains of *Xiphophorus variatus* were released in the *Xiphophorus couchianus* biotope. It is likely that tank-bred fishes were released. A similar situation exists in the Rio Purificacion, where the endemic *Xiphophorus xiphidium* population hybridizes with *Xiphophorus variatus* strains that were released there or with wild forms of *Xiphophorus variatus* that migrated in. Hybrid stocks of *Xiphophorus* were also discovered in the Rio Soto la Marina system and the Rio Guyalevo system. Natural colonization was suspected. Unfortunately, in recent years reports indicating that rare fishes have become extinct or are threatened with extinction as a result of the release of various fish species have become more freqent. Dr. Robert Rush Miller of the University of Michigan reported on one of these reprehensible machinations of faunal adulteration by so-called animal and nature lovers. According to his communication, the livebearer

*Skiffia franceasae* from the Rio Teuchitlan, Jalisco, Mexico, which was not described by Kingston until 1978, was wiped out as a result of the release of the red strain of *Xiphophorus maculatus* (red platy). It should be obvious to any animal or plant lover that he should not adulterate habitats by introducing foreign plants and animals. Species can only be preserved by protecting the biotope, whether by protecting against pollution and development or keeping away foreign animals and plants.

The yellow platy, *Xiphophorus* "*roseni,* is a natural hybrid between *X. couchianus* and *X. variatus.* Photo by L. Wischnath.

The spotted platy, *Xiphophorus* "*kosszanderi,*" is a natural hybrid. Photo by L. Wischnath.

**Many varieties of quality packaged foods are available for your fishes. Make sure that they are fed a nutritious, balanced diet.**

# Aquarium Care of the Wild Forms of the Genus *Xiphophorus*

As can be seen from the descriptions of the species and populations of the genus *Xiphophorus* in their natural habitat, they often live under conditions that differ significantly from one another with respect to water quality and temperature. In the aquarium, therefore, one should try to match the appropriate condi-

A. TWO PIECE FAUCET ADAPTOR:
   Use as needed to attach Pump (B) to any standard faucet.

B. FAUCET PUMP:
   Creates strong suction to clean. Has reverse flow feature for easy refilling.

C. OPEN/CLOSE SWITCH:
   Manually controls removal of waste and refilling with clean fresh water.

D. CLEAR GRAVEL TUBE:
   Goes into the gravel for cleaning and into the tank for refilling.

E. FDA-APPROVED, NON-TOXIC CLEAR, FLEXIBLE TUBING:
   Carries water to and from the tank.

F. SNAP CONNECTOR (OPTIONAL):
   Makes attaching the pump to the faucet a "snap".

tions as closely as possible and thereby provide the best possible care.

The members of the genus *Xiphophorus* are, in general, adaptable and long-lived charges. Regular partial water changes are a basic prerequisite for their well-being and for maintaining their health in the aquarium. Partial water changes should be carried out weekly and a third of the tank's contents should be replaced with fresh water each time. It is ad-

With an aquarium placed near a water outlet, automatic water changers can be used. These are especially suited to the swordtails and platies.

*"The members of the genus Xiphophorus are, in general, adaptable and long-lived charges."*

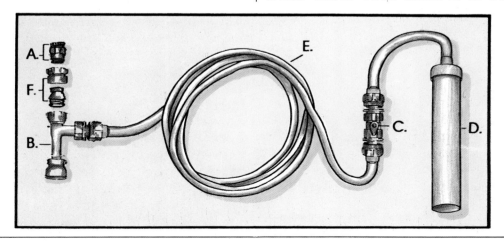

**Water quality should be monitored carefully. Test kits for pH, hardness, and chlorine/chloramine are shown here.**

**Filters not only help keep the water clean but also provide some aeration and water movement as well.**

**Chemicals that help remove unwanted ammonia and chloramine are available from your pet shop.**

visable to allow chlorinated water to stand for a while until the chlorine has evaporated unless you use a water changer. Your local petshop will have labor-saving devices to make your hobby more pleasant.

Basically, it can be said that tap water with a total hardness (dH) of between 20° and 40° is well tolerated by all species of the genus *Xiphophorus*. The pH should be alkaline, *i.e.*, between 7.5 and 8.1. A suitable water temperature would be between 22° and 28° C. The majority of the species live in bodies of water with temperatures of from 24° to 27° C.

Even when several different *Xiphophorus* species are kept in the same tank, their temperature requirements still can easily be met. A sinking of the water temperature below the average values is better tolerated by all wild forms for a fairly long time than is a raising of the temperature above the usual values. One of the reasons for this is that the oxygen content of the water decreases as the temperature increases. From the biotope descriptions,

it is apparent that all species of the genus *Xiphophorus* live in bodies of water with a high oxygen content. This is also a requirement for keeping fishes in the best of health in the aquarium.

Another important part of water care is the filtering of the water through a powerful filter. To a large degree, filtration prevents the buildup of harmful substances in the aquarium water if the filter material is changed periodically at short intervals. This interval is dependent upon the size of the tank and the fish population. As a rule, the filter material should be replaced every two weeks. In addition to slowing down the deterioration of the water quality in the aquarium, a powerful filter also provides for water movement through its return flow. This, in turn, oxygenates the water. Filters with a capacity of from 200 to 300 liters per hour can be considered as useful and recommendable when the wild forms of the genus *Xiphophorus* are kept in medium-sized tanks.

Particulary suitable in this performance category are the easy-to-clean inside filters equipped with maintenance-free motors. These are chiefly suited for tanks with a capacity of from 40 to 80 liters. An outside filter, which is better suited for larger aquaria, takes more time to clean. When cleaning the filter one must be sure to clean the inlet and outlet lines as well. The outlet line, in particular, develops a layer of decom-

A nicely set up tank containing platies and swordtails.

position products, which, with increasing thickness, introduces more and more tainted material into the filter.

## Association of Species in the Aquarium

What was said about the common occurrence of *Xiphophorus* species and populations in their natural bodies of water can be practiced only in a very restricted way when keeping them in the aquarium. That is to say, an association is possible in only a few cases. After many years of observation, it can be said that a male of any *Xiphophorus* species as a rule will mate only with females of the same species when these are present together with females of one or

*"What was said about the common ocurrence of* Xiphophorus *species and populations in their natural bodies of water can be practiced only in a very restricted way when keeping them in an aquarium."*

**Internal power filters are among the newer developments for the hobbyist.**

A selection of Eheim canister filters for aquaria of all sizes.

"... it is advisable never to keep populations of the same species or even closely related species in the same tank."

Foam cartridges in power filters make good substrates for denitrifying bacteria.

more other *Xiphophorus* species. Since, however, exceptions must be reckoned with, it is advisable never to keep populations of the same species or even closely related species in the same tank. This rule especially applies to fanciers who wish to preserve pure wild forms of the genus *Xiphophorus*. In general, a *Xiphophorus helleri* population can be kept with a small *Xiphophorus* species without another thought; for example, the *Xiphophorus helleri* population from Catemaco can be kept with *Xiphophorus milleri*. These two also live together in Lake Catemaco.

Another example is the *Xiphophorus helleri* population from the Rio Atoyac with *Xiphophorus andersi* from the same river. On the other hand, it is not possible to keep *Xiphophorus cortezi* together with *Xiphophorus variatus*, which, although they occur together in the Rio Axtla, could easily mate in the limited space of the aquarium. It is particularly inadvisable to keep fishes of the so-called platy species together in the same tank.

## Spawning

In general, spawning the wild forms of the genus *Xiphophorus* presents no problems. A prerequisite, however, is that the adults are in a good state of health. This is dependent on a proper diet and on the condition of the aquarium water. Generally, a thickly planted community tank is sufficient to permit enough young to reach maturity. In this way, a certain degree of selection is ensured. The strongest of the fry can hide in sufficient numbers from any possible attacks by the adults, thereby maintaining the stock. With the species of the genus *Xiphophorus*, whether and to what degree the young are attacked by the adults is quite variable. With some species it was not observed; for example, with the smallest members of the genus

*Xiphophorus.* With others it depends greatly on diet. If this is very varied and includes frequent feedings of live food, scarcely any attention will be paid to the young. With a one-sided diet, however, the young fish will be pursued and eaten. This is especially true of Tetramin flake food. Tetramin also fouls the aquarium when overfed. Use any good brand of granulated food, or feed some 3–4 different brands.

Particularly with the rarities of the wild forms of the genus *Xiphophorus* and the species that are already threatened in the wild, it is advisable, and for the preservation of the endangered species nothing less than mandatory, to separate the pregnant female in order to rear the

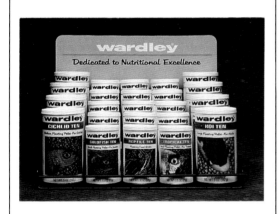

largest possible number of young. For this purpose the breeder nets and breeding traps available at your local petshop are particularly well suited. A well-filtered and well-

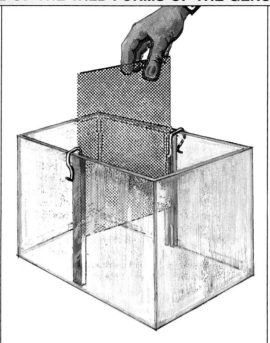

planted rearing tank should be available, in which a breeding trap with a pregnant *Xiphophorus* female is hung. The newborns can then immediately escape into the aquarium through the openings in the breeding trap.

It is important to offer optimal aquarium conditions from the birth of the young on. It is a mistake to keep growing fry in undersized tanks. They absolutely require larger tanks and a fortifying, varied diet as well as a constant water temperature. Only in this way will it be ensured that one will have fish that preserve the species under the best conditions. The serious fancier of the wild forms of the genus *Xiphophorus* will surely succeed in finding someone in

**Plastic dividers are available that fit into standard size aquaria when fish must be separated.**

**Manufacturers of fish foods commonly devise special diets for particular fishes. There are even special foods for livebearers such as platies and swordtails.**

**The correct temperature is important and many heaters, such as this submersible heater, are available.**

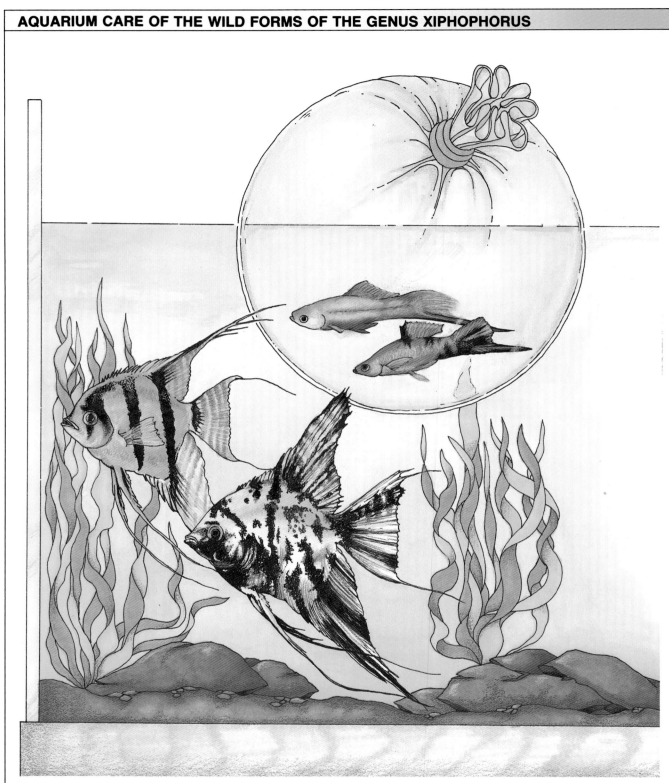

**Newly aquired fishes should be floated in the new tank so that the temperatures inside and outside of the bag can equalize.**

the circle of aquarists he knows who will be willing to take the surplus offspring, though most dealers are always eager for locally tank-raised fishes.

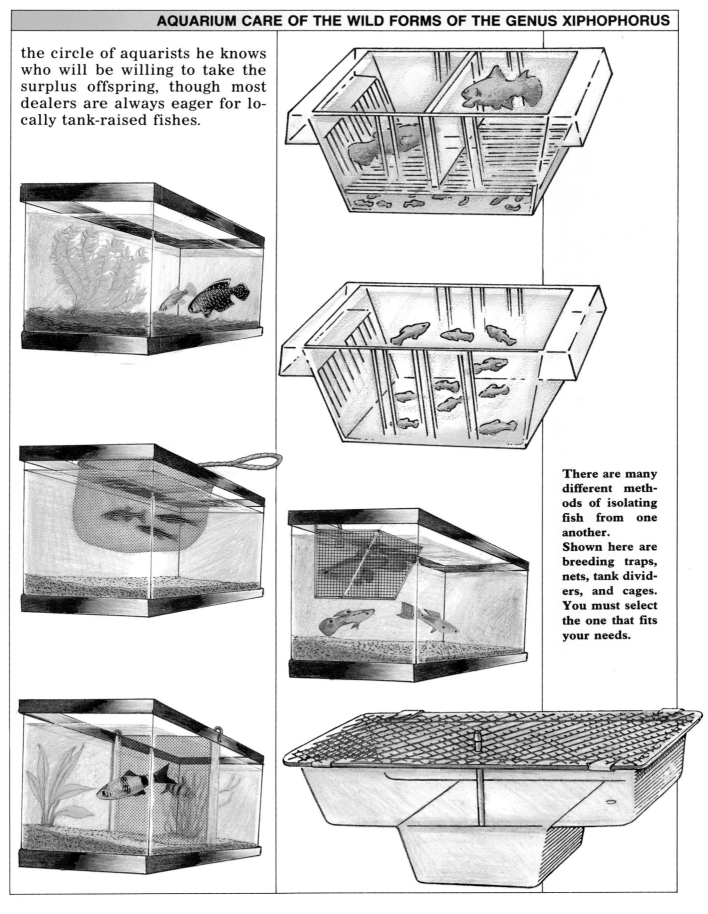

There are many different methods of isolating fish from one another. Shown here are breeding traps, nets, tank dividers, and cages. You must select the one that fits your needs.

For natural protection for livebearer babies the aquarium should be heavily planted. Seen here are *Hygrophila, Cryptocoryne* (2 species), *Cardamine*, and *Ambulia*. Photo by A. van den Nieuwenhuizen.

## The Planting of a *Xiphophorus* Aquarium

The planting of a *Xiphophorus* aquarium is governed by its purpose. It is also dependent on the fishes kept in it. Most aquaria are community and decorative tanks. In these, most aquarists strive for the so-called Dutch aquarium type; that is, grouping many species of plants that harmonize well with one another in respect to size, growth habit, leaf structure, and color. For aquaria with livebearing toothcarps all familiar floating, marsh, and aquatic plants are suitable. Very suitable for these fishes are plants that form dense tangles and which need not necessarily root in the substrate. These are sometimes called "bunch" plants since they are sold in bunches. They offer the fry excellent refuges for escaping predation by the adults.

Particularly recommended are *Najas*, *Elodea*, *Egeria*, and *Ceratophyllum* species. Generally speaking, aquaria of any size should be planted as follows:

Upward growing and tall plants should always be planted in back and along the sides. Plants with a spreading growth habit and medium-sized species should be planted in the middle

A beautifully planted and landscaped community tank. Even so, livebearer babies would be hard put to escape the predations of the angelfish. Photo by B. Kahl.

*Bunch plants: plants that form dense tangles and need not necessarily root in the substrate; usually sold in "bunches."*

The more bushy type plants the better the chances for livebearer babies to survive. Photo by W. Tomey.

Different plants create a different aspect to your tanks. The selection is primarily yours to make. Photo by A. van den Nieuwenhuizen.

Platies and swordtails in a tank exclusively decorated with plastic plants and a ceramic "log."

of the tank. The monotony of the planting of the middle of the tank can be broken with a group of tall plants. It is also possible, if the tank is large enough, to place one or more solitary plants in the middle. It is best to plant the foreground with low species, preferably those that form runners. Very effective arrangements can be achieved with the genus *Cryptocoryne*, as this genus contains a large number of species of different sizes for planting the background, middle, and foreground. Planting should never be done at random. Plenty of ideas can be found in books on aquarium decoration or aquarium plants. When planting an aquarium, it is essential to obtain information on the characteristics and care of the plants. You should make sure that the large species do not shade out smaller ones, as these may die because of lack of light. If a species of floating plant takes over the tank, it can gradually reduce the essential light reaching the rooted plants so that their continued existence becomes questionable.

The amount of light reaching all regions of the tank is kept

Four aquascapes shown in frontal and top views to show how different scenes can be created with different plant species and placements. **C** = *Cabomba*; **CB** = *Cryptocoryne beckettii*; **CC** = *Cryptocoryne cordata*; **F** = *Ceratopteris*; **H** = *Hygrophila*; **HG** = *Eleocharis*; **L** = *Ludwigia*; **M** = *Myriophyllum*; **S** = *Sagittaria*; **SP-** = *Echinodorus intermedius*; **V** = *Vallisneria*.

**A nicely planted tank, but there appear to be too many fish for its size.**

*Prune: to lop or cut off the superfluous parts of a plant for more shapely or better growth; to trim.*

constant by the regular pruning of fast-growing plants and through the regular removal of floating plants. Through appropriate planting, refuges should also be provided on the bottom. In the fishes presented in this book, whether the fry go to the water's surface or the bottom after leaving the mother's body varies depending on the species.

A planted aquarium needs regular maintenance. Fast-growing or even rank-growing plants require more care than do slow-growing plants. Naturally, maintenance must be performed more often with plants that grow upwards than with those that form rosettes on the bottom. Be-

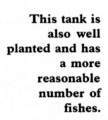

**This tank is also well planted and has a more reasonable number of fishes.**

fore planting, most of the roots should be removed from the plants. You should only leave just enough to anchor the plants in the substrate. This must be done because almost all of the old roots die after planting. They are then replaced by new roots. The old roots would become sources of decay in the substrate. With cuttings, a node must be inserted in the substrate. New roots will begin growing from this point. The leaves must first be removed from this node. With cuttings and delicate plants it is advisable to use forceps. Tubers and rhizomes can be pressed into the substrate with the fingers. Planting depth is not of particular importance. As they grow, the plants adjust their position to find the most favorable depth for themselves in the substrate.

It must be said that aquarium plants are, in general, quite adaptable in regard to temperature, water conditions, and light intensity. Among aquarists there are many who prefer the so-called biotope aquaria. This means that the tank contains fishes and plants that live together in the same bodies of water in their natural ranges.

A small species tank containing only a single species of livebearer can also be planted tastefully with one or more plant species from the same natural range. Since the natural habitats of livebearing toothcarps extend from the southern United States to South America, there are numerous ways to set up a so-called biotope aquarium. Native to this area of distribution, either individually or together, are the plant genera

A schematic view of a tank decorated with plants and driftwood.

A side view showing how taller plants are placed at the back.

Pleasing aquascapes can also be created using artificial decorations.

Planting aids for deep tanks are available.

*Elodea*, a popular and inexpensive bunch plant. Photo by G. Wolfsheimer.

*Bacopa caroliniana* is an attractive plant. Photo by Dr. D. Terver, Nancy Aquarium.

Far left: *Cabomba caroliniana* var. *multipartita.* Photo by R. Zukal.

Near left: *Ceratophyllum demersum.* Photo by R. Zukal.

*"A planted aquarium needs regular maintenance."*

*Vallisneria americana.* Cultivated and photographed by T. J. Horeman.

Above left:
Amazon sword
plant,
*Echinodorus*
sp. Photo by A.
van den
Nieuwenhuizen.

Above right:
*Echinodorus
horemani.*
Photo by R.
Zukal.

*Myriophyllum
spicatum.*
Photo by R.
Zukal.

*Echinodorus, Bacopa, Cabomba, Naja, Myriophyllum, Vallisneria, Mayaca,* and *Ceratophyllum,* to mention just the most popular. Your petshop should have many live plants from which you can choose. Many people keep aquariums just as a water garden!

The adaptability of aquatic plants in regard to temperature has already been mentioned. Nevertheless, several other observations must be made. The temperature requirements of aquarium plants are determined by the conditions in their homelands. Often, data are lacking on this, particularly concerning variations in the native bodies of water. There are tropical bodies of water that exhibit relatively high and constant temperatures throughout the entire year. As a rule, plants are kept under conditions of this kind in aquaria. Considerable seasonal temperature variations are prevalent in subtropical regions. The temperatures in

*Bacopa monniera.* **Photo by R. Zukal.**

*"The temperature requirements of aquarium plants are determined by the conditions in their homelands."*

*Cryptocoryne bullosa* **var.** *bullosa* **from a Bornean collection growing emersed in a greenhouse. Photo by T. J. Horeman.**

97

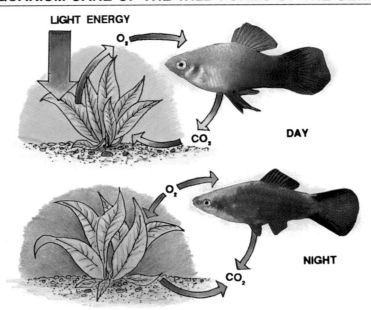

LIGHT ENERGY

$O_2$

$CO_2$

DAY

$O_2$

$CO_2$

NIGHT

Fishes, like the platy, interact with plants through both respiration and the nitrogen cycle. These interactions differ by night from those by day.

mountains of both tropical and subtropical regions are considerably lower than at lower elevations. The greatest seasonal and daily temperature fluctuations are found in very shallow and standing bodies of water. Large temperature variations both upward and downward do not injure plants in the aquarium.

In aquarium culture, however, the temperature must be adjusted specifically to the fishes in the tank. The selection of the aquarium planting must actually be determined by this. The plants themselves allow a variation of the temperature limits in both directions. Nevertheless, all environmental conditions interact in a complex way in the aquarium. The correct temperature can only have the proper effect on the plants when the light and nutrient supply are also optimal. If temperatures are kept too low for a fairly long time, the plants will exhibit dropped leaves and lack of growth. These are the first signs of the die off that will follow. If plants are kept for a fairly long time at too high a temperature, they begin to exhibit symptoms that resemble those of light deficiency: the leaf axils become longer and longer and the internodes become too long as well. Planting pots are the ideal. Developed by Holger Windelov in Denmark, his *Tropica* plants are now the world's standard.

As a general principle, in an aquarium for livebearing toothcarps the plants will tolerate

Various thermometers are available. One of the popular varieties is this digital thermometer in the form of a flat strip that has an adhesive back for attachment to the glass side of the tank.

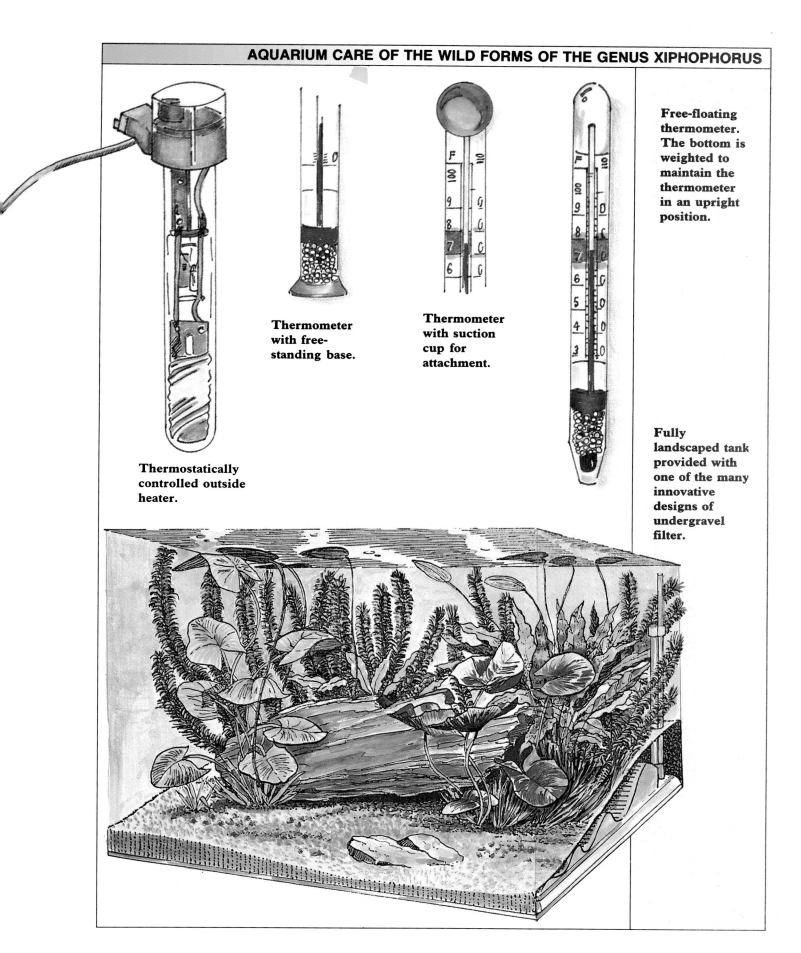

Thermostatically controlled outside heater.

Thermometer with free-standing base.

Thermometer with suction cup for attachment.

Free-floating thermometer. The bottom is weighted to maintain the thermometer in an upright position.

Fully landscaped tank provided with one of the many innovative designs of undergravel filter.

temperatures of between 20° and 25° C, whereby 20° C is the minimum for tropical and subtropical plants. A temperature of 30° C should be considered as the maximum. It makes no sense to maintain higher temperatures than this. Soon after planting an aquarium you will notice that the condition of the plants is sometimes very variable. Luxuriantly growing stands or individual plants will be noticed. Some plants will, however, also exhibit deficient growth. For this reason, patience is needed after planting an aquarium. All possible intermediate conditions between the two extremes can occur, but potted plants are almost always successful.

**Many different arrangements can be effected with an assortment of plants. Note that the gravel slopes toward the front of the tank.**

**A major step forward in keeping live plants was made by Holger Windelov of TROPICA ApS, Denmark, in which the plants are grown hydroponically and sold potted, ready for planting.**

# REPRODUCTIVE BIOLOGY AND SELECTIVE BREEDING

At the beginning of this chapter, two questions are raised immediately: 1) What are strains? and 2) How do strains differ from wild forms? By definition a strain is a line of fishes developed in captivity that has undergone a change in genetic material. The basis for this usually is the selective breeding for the desired genes. Strains, on the one hand, can be the result of hybrids between two or more species, subspecies, or races. On the other hand, changes in characters caused by mutations are genetically stable only in few cases. Mutated characters may be visible immediately or may also be masked. A spontaneous change can result from the use of specific chemicals, high temperatures, and many other things. One then speaks of a mutation if the genome of the gametes has also been altered. The basis for a species cross, in contrast to a mutation, is the introduction of new genes. The

smallest unit is the supplying of a single new hereditary factor, such as may exist in a closely inbred line.

The offspring of wild parents are called wild form offspring.

That it is possible to keep wild forms and strains for many years in the aquarium virtually unchanged in appearance and behavior is proved to us by the fishes from the stocks collected by the well-known American geneticist, Dr. Myron Gordon, and his student, Dr. Herbert R. Axelrod. His *Xiphophorus* stocks, which were in part collected in the wild in the 1930s, continue to be bred worldwide in institutions as well as by individual ex-

otic-fish fanciers and fish farmers.

It should be mentioned that all living organisms are constantly subject to small as well as large genetic changes. For this reason, it is not possible to maintain one-hundred-per cent genetic purity of various animal forms over a very long time.

## The Storage of Sperm

Of the greatest significance for selective breeding with the genus *Xiphophorus* is the storage of

The black platy (*Xiphophorus variatus*) with the reddish tail fin is very attractive but, unfortunately, not commonly available. Photo by B. Kahl.

Left: Marigold swordtails, *Xiphophorus helleri*. A male can be seen approaching a female in preparation for impregnating her. Photo by B. Kahl.

Close-up of the gonopodium of a male *Xiphophorus helleri*. Photo by M. Brembach.

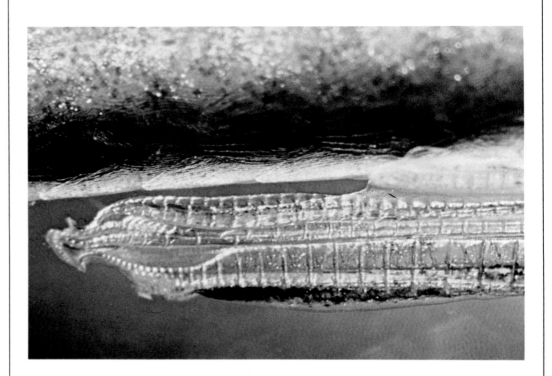

Developing embryos of *Xiphophorus helleri*.

A red-finned green swordtail, *Xiphophorus helleri*. Photo by L. Wischnath.

sperm by females. This is called "superfoetation." The result of this is that females that have been fertilized once are capable of producing young virtually their entire lives. Scientific studies have shown that the sperm can be stored in the folds of the oviducts of the female fishes. As a result, with the representatives of the genus *Xiphophorus* five to nine consecutive broods may be produced from one fertilization, which can extend over a period of one to two years.

According to Breider (1934), with our swordtails and platies there exists a definite regularity in the sequence of fertilization of the earliest and latest introduced sperm. Thus, the percentage of offspring from the second, third, and subsequent fertilizations increases steadily with each brood.

Virtually the same result holds true with all other livebearing fishes of the subfamily Poeciliinae. With the guppy, based on information from Hildemann and Wagner (1954), the sperm introduced last is supposed to overlay almost completely the sperm from earlier fertilizations, but here too a few

*Superfoetation: the storage of sperm by females, resulting in* Xiphophorus *in the production of up to nine broods by a female from a single fertilization.*

A red wag lyretail strain of swordtail is one of the fancier strains available. Photo by B. Kahl.

**This is one of the more colorful strains of *Xiphophorus variatus* and is called the parrot variatus platy in some areas.**

**An unusually colored strain of swordtail (*Xiphophorus helleri*) with bluish black body and red fins. Photo by B. Kahl.**

fry from earlier matings are occasionally observed. As a practical rule for selective breeding with the genus *Xiphophorus*, it should follow from this that sexually mature males must never be kept together with fry. Sexually mature and ripe females, which have not been fertilized by a male, periodically release infertile eggs. So far the time interval that results from this remains unexplained.

## Hybrids of the Genus *Xiphophorus*

The *Xiphophorus* strains that are available to aquarists today have resulted almost exclusively from the hybridization of three species, namely *Xiphophorus helleri*, *Xiphophorus maculatus*, and *Xiphophorus variatus*. The other members of the genus have been used only rarely for cross-breeding.

Up to now more than 60,000 *Xiphophorus* have been caught in the wild. Natural hybrids have been observed only rarely. The reasons for this are, first of all, that the individual species seldom inhabit the same region. In the Rio Axtla, Mexico, three *Xiphophorus* species live together: *Xiphophorus pygmaeus*, *Xiphophorus cortezi*, and *Xiphophorus variatus*. Each of the three species, however, favors different habitats and thus occupy different ecological niches. *Xiphophorus cortezi* prefers the deep sections of water, *Xiphophorus variatus* generally lives near the thickly grown riparian regions, and *Xiphophorus pygmaeus* is often found under steep, undercut banks.

The second important isolating mechanism is sperm competition in the individual species. In a study in 1964, Zander proved that the sperm of the same species is predominantly preferred. In the wild, *Xiphophorus* species are additionally isolated from one another through different behavior patterns. The males of every individual species possess precisely determined and genetically stable courtship behavior. Courtship serves to stimulate the female. Thus, through the male's appropriate reproductive behavior the female can be prevented from taking flight, which will ensure that a successful fertilization will take place. From laboratory experiments it is known that hybrids, in part, exhibit abnormal behavior and, in many cases, delayed sexual maturity. Some hybrids develop abnormalities of the gonopodium or fatal pigmentation (melanomas). Were such forms to appear in the wild, they would scarcely have any chance of surviving over many generations and of establishing themselves.

In the aquarium such hybrid products are selected out and are not used for further breeding. But the question also arises as to why hybrids between species do in fact occur quite frequently in the aquarium. If one gives the fishes no opportunity to choose a mate from their own

*"The Xiphophorus strains that are available to aquarists today have resulted almost exclusively from the hybridization of three species, namely Xiphophorus helleri, Xiphophorus maculatus, and Xiphophorus variatus."*

**Platies that have some swordtail blood in them usually show this by some modification of the lower edge of the caudal fin. Photo by K. Quitschau.**

The Berlin swordtail is one of the older platy/swordtail crosses. The sword is medium in size. Photo by A. van den Nieuwenhuizen.

*Chromosome: the complex, threadlike structures that carry the linearly arranged genetic units.*

*Autosomes: any chromosome other than the sex chromosome.*

species, then sexually frustrated males, in particular, will mate with females of other species. The females cannot escape from the male in the limited space of the aquarium and, in most cases, are pursued by the male until mating occurs. Once the first hybrid offspring have been obtained, it is a simple matter to mate the hybrids with one another. If active, healthy, and attractive *Xiphophorus* hybrids are desired, however, the breeder must familiarize himself with several important genetic rules.

## The Sex Chromosomes

Successful results from the crossbreeding of different *Xiphophorus* species can be achieved only when the breeder directs his attention to the sex chromosomes and the laws of inheritance. The so-called genotypic sex determination is found in most *Xiphophorus* species and will be discussed first. In the genotypic sex determining mechanism two chromosomes generally are present. They are different than the remaining chromosomes. Different forms of sex chromosomes are recognized. They are called X chromosomes and Y chromosomes. The XY type results when the female, who has two identical sex chromosomes, XX, and the male has two different ones, XY mate. Of the known *Xiphophorus* species, twelve are of the XY type.

The WZ type is a very rare form of sex determination. Here the females possess two different sex chromosomes, namely W and Z, and the males two identical ones, ZZ. *Xiphophorus maculatus* is the only species in the genus that may exhibit this sex-determining mechanism. In the cases observed so far, all *Xiphophorus maculatus* from Mexico are of the XY type. *Xiphophorus maculatus* from Honduras, Belize, and Guatemala belong to the WZ type.

The remaining members of the genus *Xiphophorus*, namely *Xiphophorus helleri*, *Xiphophorus signum*, *Xiphophorus alvarezi*, and *Xiphophorus clemenciae*, possess no sex chromosomes. Their sex is determined by the *autosomes*. All of the chromosomes other than the sex chromosomes are called *autosomes* or body cells. Here the so-called sex factors are spread over many chromosomes. For the formation of the male sex, M factors are needed. It should be noted that this type of sex determination is very unstable and can easily be disrupted and influenced by various outside influences.

Let us now turn to the inheritance of sex chromosomes. The gametes, egg cells in the female and sperm cells in the male, contain only half the full complement of chromosomes. Our

*Xiphophorus* males, with the exception of the southern *Xiphophorus maculatus*, produce two kinds of gametes or sperm cells: sperm cells that contain one Y chromosome and sperms cells that contain one X chromosome. Females only produce egg cells that contain an X chromosome. This is reversed with the southern platy. Here the males only produce sperm cells with Z chromosomes while the females produce two different ones, namely Z and W egg cells.

The sex of the offspring is determined at the time of fertilization. If the male possesses the XY sex-determining mechanism, then it establishes the sex of the offspring, since the male produces the male-determining Y sperm cells and the female-determining X sperm cells. When the male and female mate, in most cases an average of 50% female and 50% male offspring are produced.

If we mate a southern *Xiphophorus maculatus* male with ZZ sex chromosomes with a northern *Xiphophorus maculatus* female with XX chromosomes, then the first generation offspring all receive the combination ZX and all of them are males. The Z chromosome, like the Y chromosome, determines the male sex, although it is considerably weaker in its effect.

In the next example, we cross a WZ female from British Honduras with an XY male from Mexico and obtain the following sexes: 25% WX females, 25% WY males, 25% ZX males, and 25% ZY males, whereby the WY and ZX males are considered to be unstable.

Only the experienced breeder should attempt matings between

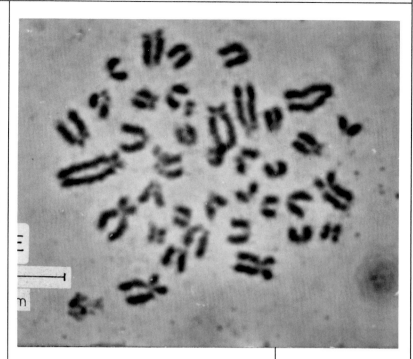

Dividing chromosomes during the metaphase of *Aphyosemion puerzli*, a killifish. Photo by J. J. Scheel.

the two different sex types. A beginner can easily lose control and finally will no longer be sure which of his hybrids belongs to which type.

Let us now turn to the *Xiphophorus helleri* hybrids. All species of the *Xiphophorus helleri* complex possess, as was already mentioned, no sex chromosomes at all. So we will now produce a hybrid of the combination of a female *Xiphophorus helleri* and a male *Xiphophorus maculatus* with ZZ sex chromosomes. Since we now know that *Xiphophorus helleri* has no sex chromosomes, we will not be too surprised when the offspring are equally divided between males and females. If we, however, cross an XX *Xiphophorus maculatus* female with a male *Xiphophorus helleri*, we obtain only female fish. With the *Xiphophorus helleri* hybrids it becomes clear that without knowledge of important facts, successful selective breeding in the genus *Xiphophorus* will be virtually impossible.

*"The sex of the offspring is determined at the time of fertilization."*

107

A breeding file is highly recommended so that the breeder can keep track of the different crosses. Photo of a female swordtail, *Xiphophorus helleri*, by R. Zukal.

## Maintaining a Breeding File

The first step when starting the successful selective breeding of *Xiphophorus* is to list all of the data of a breeding line in a chart. We start by numbering each individual fish that is to be used for selective breeding. Our goal will be the crossing of two *Xiphophorus* lines, which differ in a pair of color alleles.

As the progenitor, we choose an albino *Xiphophorus helleri* male and give him the breeding number 001. The ancestress, a normal wild-colored green female, receives the number 002. Accordingly, the page in the file is labelled with the designation 001/002 and receives the following parental data: source of the fish; description of color; mated on; date of first, second, third . . . brood; onset of sexual maturity in the offspring; end of sexual maturity; colors of the offspring; date of death. Depending on one's requirements, other data can be listed in the file.

*"The first step when starting the successful selective breeding of* Xiphophorus *is to list all of the data of a breeding line in a chart."*

A magnificent prize-winning male albino swordtail, *Xiphophorus helleri*. Photo by Dr. H. Grier.

## Inheritance

We will now follow the mating of 001/002. With the newborns of the first brood we already determine that none of the fish possesses the typical red eyes of albinos. What has happened?

Before we can answer this question we must first briefly discuss cell structure. The cell is the smallest living unit. All organisms are made up of one or more cells and each one of the cells has the same genotype. Consequently, all cells could in theory be used for reproduction; however, with fishes, in the same way as with people, special female and male gametes are used for this purpose. A natural prerequisite for the creation of a new life with fishes is almost exclusively the fusion of egg and sperm cells (both of which are gametes). The chromosomes are found in every cell nucleus. In contrast to the somatic (body) cells, the gametes contain only half the full complement of chromosomes. The half complement of chromosomes is 23 in human beings and 24 in the individual *Xiphophorus* species.

All of the hereditary factors lie in sequence on the chromosomes and are called *genes*. In a stricter sense it is actually the genes that determine the genetic characters. Several genes take part in the formation of the familiar sword in *Xiphophorus helleri* males. Other factors, on the other hand, are determined by only a single gene.

In the fusion of the egg and sperm cells, as was previously mentioned, the half complements of chromosomes are brought together so that the fer-

This is a male pearl albino platy. Photo by Dr. J. Norton.

*"Several genes take part in the formation of the familiar sword in* Xiphophorus helleri *males."*

Genotype: the genetic constitution of an organism, usually in respect to one or only a few genes relevant in a particular context.

tilized (egg) cell again has the full complement of chromosomes. In the genus *Xiphophorus* the number is 48 per somatic cell, or 24 per germ (sex) cell.

Let us now continue with our sample cross and give the swordtail pair suitable symbols for their body-color characters. The pure green *Xiphophorus helleri* female receives the symbol **AA** for its ground color, and we give the pure albino male the symbol **aa**. We know that the chromosomes, and in our two fishes the designated color gene as well, are found in a double dose in the somatic cells. For this reason we need to use two symbols. In all cases only one letter is needed for the egg and sperm cells, the germ cells. Now we choose one egg cell from the green wild-colored *Xiphophorus* female and symbolize the dominant green color by **A**. The sperm cell of the albino male is symbolized by **a**, which reflects the recessive albino color. Both gametes fuse at the time of fertilization. In our case a new type is produced, namely a type **Aa**

A Punnett square showing the crossing of a pure green female *Xiphophorus helleri* swordtail (AA) with a pure albino male (aa). This results in 100% heterozygous progeny (Aa) that are green like the mother.

|  ♀ ♂ | **A** | **A** |
|---|---|---|
| **a** | **Aa** | **Aa** |
| **a** | **Aa** | **Aa** |

*Bottom left:* Crossing the heterozygotes (Aa X Aa) produces 25% pure albinos (aa), 25% pure greens (AA), and 50% heterozygotes (Aa).

*Bottom right:* If a heterozygous (Aa) female is mated with a pure albino male (aa), there should be 50% heterozygotes (Aa) and 50% homozygous albinos (aa).

fish. It appears green because of the dominance of the wild color, but, nevertheless, carries the albino character from the father even though it is not visible. Therefore, a heterozygous (mixed) *Xiphophorus helleri* has been created. In this example, Mendel's first law (the law of segregation) is in operation. But how do we again obtain albino fish? We simply cross our **Aa** offspring with one another and obtain the second generation ($F_2$) with the following combinations:

25% of all $F_2$ fish are homozygous (pure) albinos with the genetic formula **aa**;

25% of all $F_2$ fish are homozygous green *Xiphophorus* with the genetic formula **AA**;

50% of all $F_2$ fish are heterozygous green swordtails with the genetic formula **Aa**.

Therefore, we obtained a ratio of 1 : 2 : 1. In this instance it is a question of Mendel's second law (law of independent assortment).

In order to build up a large stock of pure albinos, we now need to mate our pure **aa** fish with one another. When we do this, we will always obtain only albinos. To increase the number of albinos in the $F_2$ generation, we also could have backcrossed the offspring with their father. If a heterozygous **Aa** is mated with the pure **aa** albino father we can expect a result of 50% **Aa** and 50% **aa** fish. In this case, however, we would not have any pure green swordtails. Mendel's second law (the law of independent assortment) also concerns those cases of inheritance in which a hereditary factor is distinguished by two or more character pairs.

| ♂ ♀ | **A** | **a** |
|---|---|---|
| **A** | **AA** | **Aa** |
| **a** | **Aa** | **aa** |

| ♀ ♂ | **A** | **a** |
|---|---|---|
| **a** | **Aa** | **aa** |
| **a** | **Aa** | **aa** |

Until now we have discussed genes that differ only in one character pair. This is called *monohybrid* inheritance. Now we will produce a very rare *Xiphophorus* strain, the gold-albino swordtail. Since we obtained only a single male, we mated the treasure with a green *Xiphophorus helleri* female. In the $F_1$ generation we obtain, in accordance with Mendel's first law, only green *Xiphophorus helleri*. Now we cross the $F_1$ generation with one another and obtain the second generation with the following result: statistically, of 16 offspring we obtain nine green *Xiphophorus helleri*, three golden *Xiphophorus helleri*, three albino *Xiphophorus helleri*, and one golden-albino *Xiphophorus helleri*, a ratio of 9 : 3 : 3 : 1. From the cross of golden-albino X green two additional color types, namely gold-colored and albino-colored, were produced.

## Inbreeding

In aquarium fish breeding, by inbreeding one means the mating of brother and sister, mother and son, or father and daughter. However, the spectrum of inbreeding also reveals itself in further gradations. The strictest possiblity is self-fertilization,

An albino swordtail/platy cross (note the short sword). The pink eyes identify the true albino. Photo by Dr. H. R. Axelrod.

*"In aquarium fish breeding, by inbreeding one means the mating of brother and sister, mother and son, or father and daughter."*

Albinos can be developed in all fancy strains of swordtail. This is an albino lyretail swordtail. Photo by Dr. H. R. Axelrod.

The small fish is a male *X. maculatus* from Rio Jamapa with a gene for spotted dorsal and one for red dorsal and anal fins. The large fish is a female *X maculatus* X *X. helleri* hybrid with the same genes. Photo by K. Kallman.

*"Experiments of long standing show that close inbreeding combined with planned selective breeding produces first-class fishes in swordtails and platies."*

which, however, appears only extremely rarely in the genus *Xiphophorus* and which scarcely can be influenced. The designation *close inbreeding* refers to the crossing of parents and offspring or between offspring. The third gradation level of inbreeding is represented by moderate inbreeding. Here matings between half brothers and half sisters as well as between cousins come into consideration. Under the designation *loose inbreeding* one understands the crossing of more distant relatives.

In human beings, in particular, there are countless examples that, in most cases, inbreeding leads to inheritable defects of the organism. The result is quite different with inbreeding in fishes. Experiments of long standing show that close inbreeding combined with planned selective breeding produces first-class fishes in swordtails and platies. Without inbreeding, selective breeding would be unimaginable with fishes. The best poultry or the most productive vegetables are

First generation *X. helleri* X *X. maculatus* hybrid (note the short sword). The black spots are from the swordtail, the red color from the platy. Photo by K. Kallman.

*Xiphophorus variatus* **albino male. Photo by Dr. H. R. Axelrod.**

the result of two inbred lines, which over many generations have been bred into two different lines.

## Line Breeding

Line breeding can be considered as very profitable. Here we are dealing with the mating of closely related fish. In the first tank the progenitor is kept with several well-developed daughters (females). The offspring are subsequently reared in a separate tank. Later the two best pairs are taken from there. Each pair is kept separately in two different tanks for further breeding. The offspring of both pairs are again separated and reared to maturity in rearing tanks. We have now obtained two separate lines. Generation after generation the lines continue to be bred in brother and sister lines. Now one must care-

fully make sure that both separate lines are equally well developed and that they do not diverge from each other after several generations. In a blood red platy stock all lines must be bright-red colored, including the eye ring. In a golden *Xiphophorus helleri* stock, both lines must develop the golden color.

After the eighth generation (F_8) the two lines can be mated with each other. Now more aquaria will be needed. Under certain circumstances, a line that has grown weaker should be maintained until it becomes clear whether the crossing has been successful. As has already been discovered by some fish breeders, there is no better experience than to maintain first-class fishes over a long period of time. Often as many as three or four lines are produced from a valuable line.

*". . . a line that has grown weaker should be maintained until it becomes clear whether the crossing has been successful."*

*Line breeding: the mating of closely related fish generation after generation.*

A strain of *Xiphophorus maculatus* called the sunburst platy. Photo by Dr. W. E. Burgess.

A pair of cherry red platies, *Xiphophorus maculatus*. Photo by G. Wolfsheimer.

## Building Up and Maintaining Breeding Stocks

In ornamental-fish breeding, various methods are used to maintain or improve particular strains. In the main, these are inbreeding, line breeding, and backcrossing. In inbreeding, close, moderate, and loose inbreeding are distinguished. By close inbreeding is meant the mating of father and daughter, mother and son, or sister and brother. In these matings the percentage of identical genes is very high. In practice this means that the fishes not only look identical, but they also pass on identical characters to their offspring.

In moderate inbreeding, half-brothers and half-sisters or cousins are mated with each other. Here the percentage of identical genetic characters is reduced. If distantly related fishes are crossed, this is called loose inbreeding. Accordingly, the percentage of identical genetic information is even less.

Through inbreeding it is possible to produce homozygous or genetically pure fishes. This can, however, also have negative consequences; for example, deformities of the spine can appear, since in general inbreeding leads to the loss of vitality and fertility if populations are allowed to breed without restriction. For this reason it is essential to perform strict, planned selection on the offspring. In the guppy, swordtail, or platy, inbreeding leads to selectively bred fishes, as is shown by long-term experiments. It is even possible to go so far as to say that successful selective breeding is impossible without inbreeding. A wonderful book on guppy breeding was written by Iwasaki in 1989.

In animal and plant breeding, it is usual today to simultaneously breed several inbred stocks. If two of these inbred stocks are then crossed with each other, the so-called heterosis effect may appear in the $F_1$ generation. Heterosis is the

*"Through inbreeding it is possible to produce homozygous or genetically pure fishes."*

The two species of platy commonly used for crossbreeding in the hobby to produce colorful strains. Above is *Xiphophorus maculatus,* below is *Xiphophorus variatus.* Photos by B. Kahl.

strengthening of a desired character. These $F_1$ hybrids are usually also more resistant to diseases and are more vigorous. It must not be forgotten, however, that this effect diminishes again in the following generations. Therefore, in general it is not worthwhile to breed $F_1$ hybrids. We can also achieve the same effect by crossing fishes of the same strain from a different breeder's stocks into our stock. Breeders formerly called this bringing in new blood. Geneticists call this phenomenon "hybrid vigor."

The most extreme case of inbreeding is self-fertilization. This, however, does not occur in the genus *Xiphophorus*. In this connection, attention is drawn to the natural hybrids of *Poecilia formosa*. Only females are found in this species. These hybrids are produced by a cross between *Poecilia mexicana* and *Poecilia latipinna*.

As we have already seen in the section on inbreeding, it is worthwhile to breed several lines of a strain. It is most practical to proceed as follows in line breeding: the chosen progenitor is mated with several of his daughters. From the offspring, the same number of pairs as the number of desired lines are selected. Each pair now forms the foundation for one inbred line. The offspring of the individual pairs are now kept separately. In the following generations it is advisable always to mate brother and sister.

The development of the individual lines should be monitored closely and the strictest selection should be performed. In addition, the individual lines must not be allowed to deviate from one another in the desired characters. After about eight to ten generations the different lines can be crossed with one another. A new line is then established with these fish and the weakest of the old lines can be

*Heterosis: the strengthening of a desired character; also sometimes known as hybrid vigor when crossing fishes of the same strain from a different breeder's stock into your own stock.*

**It is generally necessary to breed two or more lines so that the strain can be invigorated when the straight line breeding causes degeneration of the strain. Photo by B. Kahl.**

*Backcross: when the offspring are crossed with one of the parents.*

**Backcrossing is chiefly used when characters or colors displayed only in the parents need to be strengthened in the offspring. Shown is *X. helleri*.**

allowed to die out. In order to achieve first-class fishes with livebearers over a fairly long time, you will have no choice but to maintain several lines of a stock.

In the backcross, the offspring are crossed with one of the parents; that is, daughter with father or son with mother. It is chiefly used when color or form characters that are displayed only by the parents are to be strengthened in the offspring. It is known from individual representatives of the genus *Xiphophorus* that areas of color can be strengthened or weakened by simple backcrossing. The intense red- or black-colored strains of *Xiphophorus* were developed in this way. The percentage of homozygous fishes can be increased by backcrossing the heterozygous offspring with a homozygous parent.

The color of this strain of swordtails has been enhanced but at the cost of the length of the male's sword. Photo by A. Roth.

This will be demonstrated through the example of the hereditary factor for the spotted dorsal (**Sd**) color gene. The Sd hereditary factor is responsible for one or more black spots in the dorsal fin of *Xiphophorus maculatus*. This color gene occurs in a few populations of *Xiphophorus maculatus*. If a *Xiphophorus maculatus* with the Sd color is crossed with a swordtail that does not have this gene, in the $F_1$ fish are obtained in which these black spots are clearly larger and which also spread onto the body. If these $F_1$ fish are again crossed with a swordtail, the most variable fish are obtained. In this so-called $F_2R$ there are now fish that do not exhibit any black spots, those that have experienced a further increase in the black pigmentation, and those that develop malignant melanomas. The degree of expression of the melanoma can be very variable. Some fish die after several months, while others can reach sexual maturity and even reproduce.

If these tumor-carrying fish are now backcrossed with *Xiphophorus maculatus* lacking the Sd color gene, the following picture emerges: In the $F_1$ the heavy pigmentation is suppressed and the melanoma is no longer malignant. If these fish are then crossed with *Xiphophorus maculatus* without the Sd color gene, a further reduction in the pigmentation results. In this $F_2$ the fish again look like normal *Xiphophorus maculatus* without the Sd color pattern.

*Melanomas: benign or malignant tumors composed of cells containing dark pigments.*

Top left: A pair of gold speckled platies, male below. Top right: A pair of speckled platies but without the strong gold coloration. Photos by Dr. H. R. Axelrod.

A hybrid *X. maculatus* X *X. helleri*. The lower edge of the tail fin has the merest indication of a sword. Photo by K. Quitschau.

A milk-and-ink hi-fin platy. Photo by G. Takeshita.

Black and red make a dramatic combination. This is commonly sought after in color strains of platies and swordtails. Photo by M. Gilroy.

*"The degree of expression of the melanoma can be very variable. Some fish die after several months, while others can reach sexual maturity and even reproduce."*

# STANDARD STRAINS OF SWORDTAILS

### *Xiphophorus helleri* Type

We strive for standards in which the body shape and size, including the sword, are completely identical with those of the wild form of *Xiphophorus helleri*.

**TOTAL LENGTH WITHOUT SWORD:**

Length of the female: 7–9 centimeters.

Length of the male: 6–8 centimeters.

**BODY GROUND COLORS:**

#### Red

Color class 1: bright, intense red. Blood red.

Color class 2: opaque red.

Color class 3: orange-red or orange.

#### Albino

Color class 1: albino red.

Color class 2: albino yellow.

Color class 3: albino white.

#### Green

Corresponds to the coloration of the wild form.

#### Gold

Color class 1: golden-red.

Color class 2: golden-yellow.

Color class 3: golden-white.

Color class 4: golden-albino.

#### Black

Corresponds to a black body color.

#### Interference colors

In all color patterns the most intense degree of color of the individual classes should be strived for. The patterns of markings must not run into one another and must form clear boundries. Interference colors generally allow no distinct demarcation and can, depending on how the light strikes, appear in various color combinations. Caudal peduncle and tail fin markings are not desired with the *Xiphophorus helleri* type.

*"In all color patterns the most intense degree of color of the individual classes should be strived for."*

**A marigold twinbar (comet) lyretail swordtail female. Photo by E. C. Taylor.**

A male red lyretail swordtail. Photo by E. C. Taylor.

A female of the same strain — red lyretail swordtail. Photo by E. C. Taylor.

A female pineapple wag lyretail swordtail. Photo by E. C. Taylor.

**FIN COLORS.**
Black, red, yellow, and clear.
Wagtail—the individual fin rays
are black.
Arnold factor—the spaces be-
tween the fin rays are black.

## Color Pattern Guidelines

The fin coloration should also
attain the most intense degree
of color. As far as possible, the
total coloration of all fin rays,
intermediate spaces, or the en-

A male red
twinbar
swordtail.
Photo by E. C.
Taylor.

A male
pineapple wag
lyretail
swordtail.
Photo by E. C.
Taylor.

A female
marigold wag
lyretail
swordtail.
Photo by E. C.
Taylor.

A mixture of fancy strains of swordtails, mostly lyretails. Photo by B. Kahl.

tire fin areas are strived for. With the wagtail color, only the fin rays are pigmented black, while the fin membranes are free of pigment. The opposite is true of the Arnold factor. Here the fin membranes are black and the fin rays remain unpigmented. The combination of wagtail and Arnold factor is possible. Completely black fins result. The males' swords may, as much as possible, be edged in black.

**FIN SHAPE.**
Group 1: normal-finned.
Group 2: high-finned.

Normal-finned fishes should be completely identical in fin shape to the wild form, in this case *Xiphophorus helleri*. The size of the sword must attain the average length of the *Xiphopho-rus helleri* wild form.

Pathologically altered or deformed fins are inadmissible. Tattered or injured fins are given a point deduction.

The high-finned fishes are classified in two fin-expression types. The lyre-fins should, as far as possible, not be bred and are not considered in this book.

**2a. FLAG FORM.** With the flag form all fin rays of the dorsal fin are elongated about threefold to fourfold and should, as far as possible, form a straight termination. The fishes can, depending on stimulation, erect the high fins. Males often possess a taller high fin than females; it is, however, allowable and does not demand a point deduction in judging. In both sexes the upper width of the fin should not differ

*Arnold factor: the fin membranes are black while the fin rays remain unpigmented.*

*Wagtail: only the fin rays are black pigmented; the fin membranes are free of color.*

significantly from the lower.

**2b. VEIL FORM.** With the veil form all fin rays are elongated about sixfold to eightfold. The veil fin should, if possible, have a straight termination. The fishes cannot completely erect the veil fin. The enormously enlarged dorsal fin should be about the same height in both males and females. The upper edge of the dorsal fin is wider than the base. The fishes must not be impeded in their movements by the veil fin.

## Fin Alterations

The first domesticated forms of the high-finned *Xiphophorus helleri* apparently first appeared in the aquarium trade in 1962 under the name Simpson helleri, which were characterized by an enormously large dorsal fin. According to the universally laid down guidelines, Simpson helleri is designated as a "hifin" today. The fishes of that time resemble today's veil forms very closely. Professor Schröder, in a

Pineapple lyretail swordtail. Photo by Dr. Harry Grier.

A male gold wag lyretail swordtail. Photo by E. C. Taylor.

A female gold wag lyretail swordtail. Photo by E. C. Taylor.

One of the platy strains with an impressive dorsal fin is the Simpson hi-fin. Photo by B. Kahl.

The brushtail platy is one of the more unusual hobby strains. Photo by B. Kahl.

scientific paper published in 1965, concerned himself specifically with the inheritance of the Simpson factor. Schröder showed that the Simpson factor causes an enlargement of the dorsal fin, although the number of fin rays does not change. When fully spread, the dorsal fin of one-year-old, sexually mature specimens of the veil form can attain five times the height of the dorsal fin of normal-finned siblings of the same age. Newborn high-fins cannot be distinguished from normal-fins.

The third dorsal fin ray starts to elongate 14 days after birth at the earliest. Only much later, after about six to eight weeks, does the elongation of the remaining rays also begin. Shortly after the onset of sexual maturity, sexually mature high-finned females can be distinguished from high-finned males. Apparently through the influence of sex hormones the male's dorsal fin exhibits a relatively narrow, banner-like form. Often the high fin grows as long as the fish's body and sometimes can even extend beyond the end of the tail. With *Xiphophorus helleri* the female's high fin, which grows to about half the body length, develops more in width than in length and exhibits more points per fin ray. Furthermore, Schröder also points out that under exactly the same rearing conditions, at high population densities, at an age of two months the normal-finned specimens can be twice as long as their high-finned siblings.

In the breeding experiments of Schröder, in the crossing Simpson helleri x *Xiphophorus maculatus*, offspring were produced that were additionally characterized by an elongated anal fin. Lyretails, which appeared later, certainly can be derived from this crossing combination. Since male lyretail fishes, because of the abnormal enlargement of the male sex organ (gonopodium), cannot reproduce on their own and exhibit an additional elongation of all fins that greatly limits their movements, they will not be discussed here.

In recent years, brush-tail platies and pointed-tail platies

The upper fish is a Mickey Mouse (complete moon) platy, the lower fish is a hi-fin red jet swordtail. Photo by Dr. H. R. Axelrod.

*"With the crossing combination of high-fin with high-fin, in a brood of 30 offspring, on average about 20 high-fins and 10 normal-fins can be expected."*

A saddleback hi-fin platy. Photo by G. Takeshita.

have been produced in fanciers' tanks. With the brush-tail platy, as well as with the pointed-tail platy, the middle tail-fin rays, as well as the pectoral fins, are about twice normal length. All other fins exhibit a normal wild-type fin development. Which genes are responsible for the two new forms has not yet been analyzed. All fin alterations, however, have one thing in common: apparently egg cells that carry the dominant hereditary factors for the formation of elongated fins cannot be fertilized by sperm cells with the same factor. Schröder considers that specific sex substances, which cause the sperm cells actively to seek out the ripe eggs, may not be produced or are produced in insufficient quantity or quality. In such cases one speaks of the incompatibility of the gametes. With the crossing combination of high-fin with high-fin, in a brood of 30 offspring, on average about 20 high-fins and 10 normal-fins can be expected.

The ratio is somewhat more favorable with the brush-tail platy, as an average of 25 brush-fins and 5 normal-fins can be expected from the combination brush-tail platy x brush-tail platy. The brush-tail has so far appeared prominently only with the *Xiphophorus maculatus* and *Xiphophorus variatus* types, whereas the high-fin is already present with all *Xiphophorus* types.

A red speckled Berlin crossbreed swordtail. Photo by B. Kahl.

*Opposite:* 1. Wagtail swordtail. 2. Berlin crossbreed. 3. Hamburg crossbreed. Photos by B. Kahl.

## The Backcross

The backcross represents the foundation of *Xiphophorus* selective breeding and, therefore, will be explained by means of a simple example.

If one mates a female and a male differing in one or more characters and belonging to the same or a different species, subspecies, or race, one designates this mating as the parental generation, symbolized by the letter P. Through the above-mentioned mating one obtains the first filial generation (abbreviated $F_1$). The $F_1$ offspring are called hybrids. If a hybrid offspring is now mated with one of the parents, one speaks of a backcross. Backcrosses are necessary when one wishes to emphasize particular color characters or body proportions, which are exclu-

sively or predominantly possessed by one of the parents. With the individual members of the genus *Xiphophorus*, it is also known that through backcrossing one can easily intensify or diminish particular color factors. Through this decisive principle alone it was possible to produce, for example, the intense red- and black-colored *Xiphophorus* strains through repeated backcrosses. (On this subject also see diseases of the genus *Xiphophorus*.)

## Berlin Crossbreed

This attractive crossbreed was first mentioned in the aquarium literature in 1916. The red body, the dorsal fin, and the tail fin are dotted with numerous dark spots. The individual spots should be well set off from one another and should exhibit a round to oval shape on the body and a comma-like shape on the fins. The male's sword should attain a length of from 3 to 4.5 centimeters and should either be completely black or edged in black.

Berlin Swordtails can be bred from various crosses. Only a few of the possible combinations will be mentioned here.

1. Green, black-speckled *Xiphophorus helleri* × red strain of *Xiphophorus helleri*.
2. Black-speckled *Xiphophorus helleri* × red strain of *Xiphophorus maculatus*.
3. Black-speckled *Xiphophorus maculatus* × red strain of *Xiphophorus helleri*.

Caution is advised with the last-mentioned cross, since a high percentage of the offspring develop melanomas. Wild forms that resemble the Berlin cross-

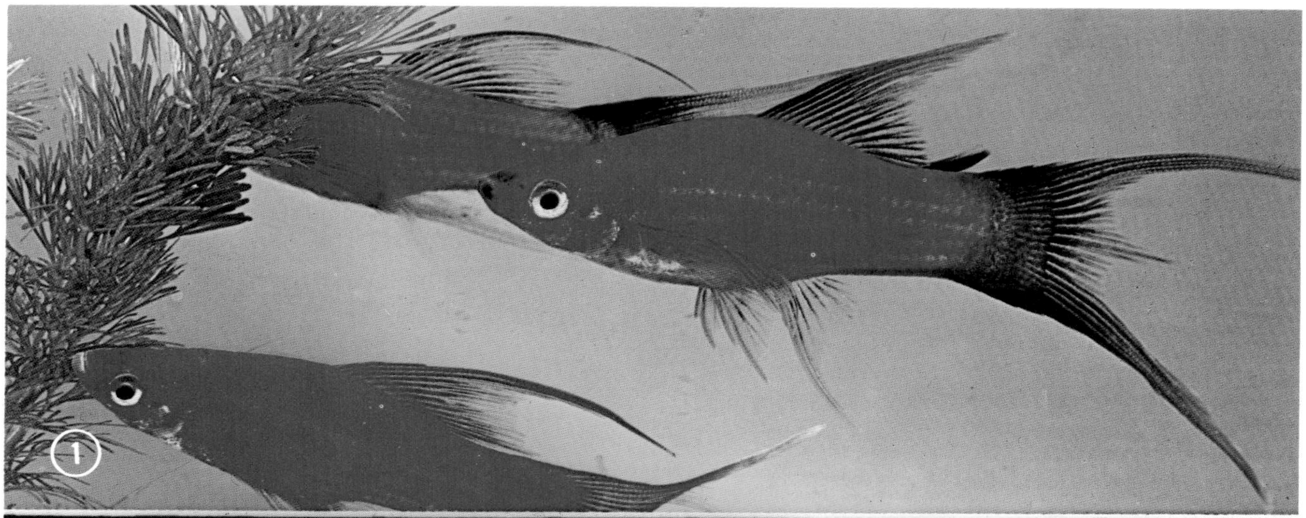
1

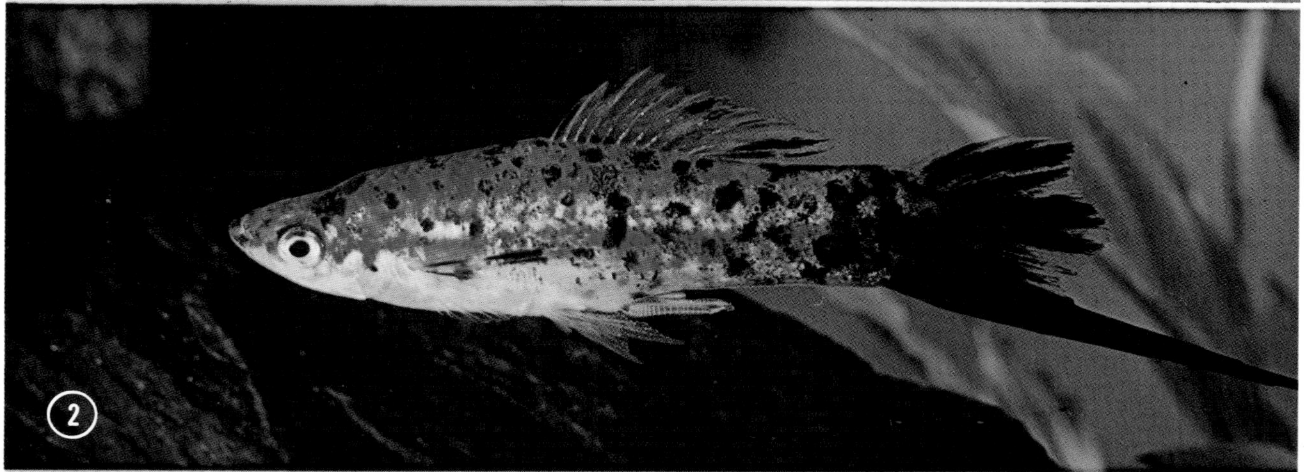
2

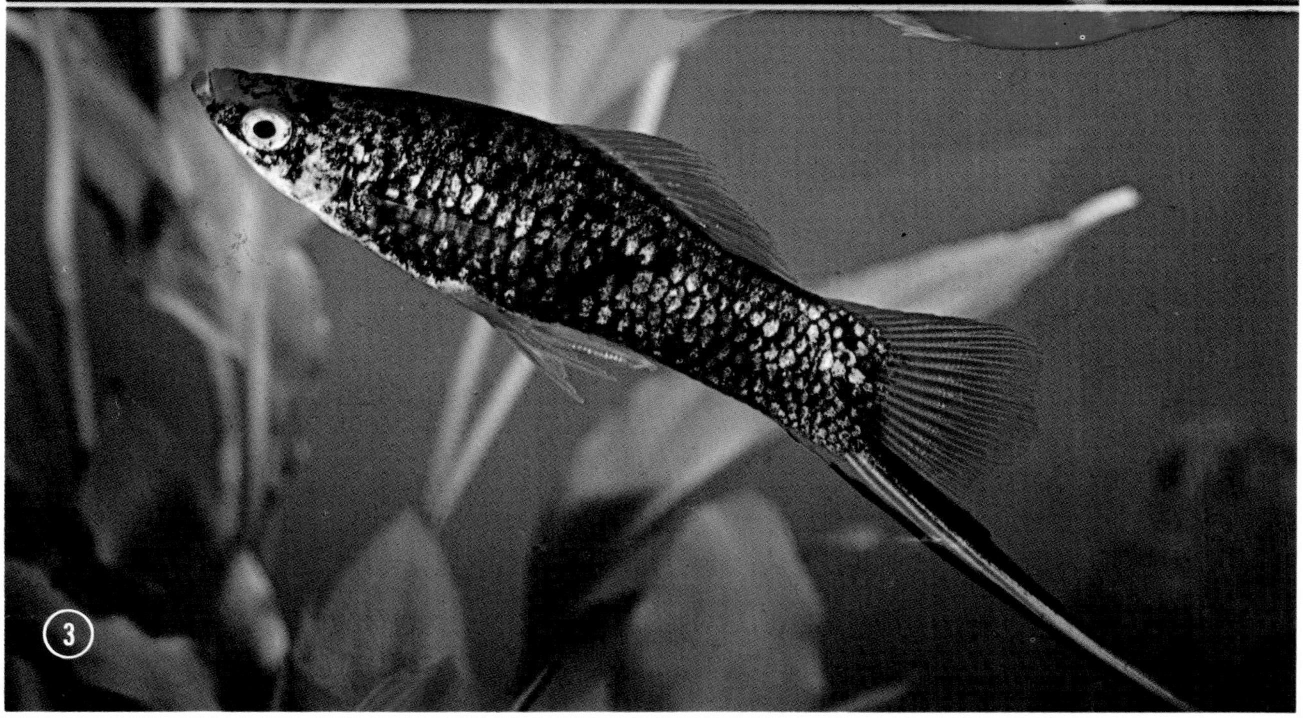
3

A spotted Berlin crossbreed with a streak of yellow in the tail. The black pigment cells will probably develop into a carcinoma. Photo by H. Hansen.

A black-and-gold lyretail swordtail. Photo by Dr. H. Grier.

A spotted, almost peppered Berlin hi-fin swordtail. Photo by K. Quitschau.

breed in appearance have occasionally been reported in the specialist literature. Several years ago Wischnath was able to furnish positive proof of black-speckled, red *Xiphophorus helleri* in the wild. He collected this beautiful wild form in the Rio Atoyac and in the Rio Playa Vicente in Mexico. By crossing this fish with the strain one can expect an improvement in the line.

## Wiesbaden Crossbreed

In 1937, in a paper in the *Wochenscrift für Aquarien- und Terrarienkunde*, Dr. H. Breider introduced the results of two new Wiesbaden breeding attempts and for the first time the Wiesbaden crossbreed, *Xiphophorus helleri* type. Dr. Mombour developed the described strains after lengthy selective breeding. This crossbreed was developed through the hybridization of a green wild-colored *Xiphophorus helleri* female with a *Xiphophorus maculatus* male of the black variety. Breider wrote the following about the Mombour specimens: One day Dr. Mombour observed two *Xiphophorus helleri* males that were black colored only on the lower body half below the red longitudinal band typical of *Xiphophorus helleri*. He crossed these males with unvariegated gray-green *Xiphophorus helleri* females. The result was that among the offspring of male number 1, which had only a few black spots, some very intensely black colored fish appeared, which are probably familiar to aquarists. The offspring of male number 2, which was intensely black colored on the ventral side of the body, were in part colored like the father. For further breeding Mombour then used the weakly black-colored fish and mated them with those females he knew belonged to a line that when mated with male number 2 produced, for the most part, only ventrally black-colored offspring. In this way Dr. Mombour finally succeeded in breeding a largely uniform new variety.

The black color of this variety, which is black on the ventral

A pair of normal finned Berlin swordtails. Photo by H. Pinter.

A pair of Wiesbaden swordtails in which the black ventral portion extends as far as the head. Photo by K. Quitschau.

half of the body, can extend up to the head. The upper half of the body remains free of the intense black color and appears gray-green. The black area can extend onto the sword in males, so that in some males the sword appears to be black colored. The black coloration is caused by only a single color factor.

The black factor, *nigra,* is dominant to green and is symbolized by a capital **N**. If one mates a pure **NN** Wiesbaden specimen with a green wild swordtail, in this case with the genetic for-

A pair of Wiesbaden crossbreeds with the black extending only as far as the ventral fins. Photo by B. Kahl.

**Another example of the Wiesbaden cross but with a lyretail.**

*Heterozygous: the condition wherein an individual has different alleles at one or more loci and therefore produces gametes of two or more different kinds.*

**Punnet Square representation of:**
**1. Pure Wiesbaden × Pure green cross.**
**2. Hybrid Wiesbaden × hybrid Wiesbaden cross.**
**3. Pure Wiesbaden × Pure Wiesbaden cross.**

mula **nn**, according to Mendel's first law one obtains heterozygous **Nn** fish. As is known, they look like the Wiesbaden crossbreed in coloration, but their hereditary factors also include the factor **n**. If we now cross heterozygous **Nn** fish with one another, **Nn × Nn**, according to Mendel's second law one obtains 25% pure Wiesbaden crossbreed specimens with the formula **NN**, 50% heterozygous **Nn** swordtails, and 25% pure green **nn** swordtails. If we then mate **NN × NN** fish, only pure Wiesbaden cross specimens result. Breider designated this fish standard as the variety *seminigra*.

Mombour also bestowed a red-black Wiesbaden line upon aquarists, which Breider writes about as follows: With the logical knowledge of the inheritance of the **N** color gene, Dr. Mombour went even further. Besides selection and inbreeding, an additional important means of obtaining new lines is through the combining of hered-

① 

|   | ♂ N | N |
|---|---|---|
| **n** | **Nn** | **Nn** |
| **n** | **Nn** | **Nn** |

② 

|   | ♂ N | n |
|---|---|---|
| **N** | **NN** | **Nn** |
| **n** | **Nn** | **nn** |

③ 

|   | ♂ N | N |
|---|---|---|
| **N** | **NN** | **NN** |
| **N** | **NN** | **NN** |

A Wiesbaden red-black strain in which the black dominates. Photo by S. Frank.

itary factors. Based on this a black **'seminigra'** male was mated with a female red swordtail.

The Wiesbaden red-blacks are black on the ventral side of the body and are red colored on the upper side of the body. However, it is not possible to breed this color variety as a pure strain, since the red factor **R** is an allele of the black factor **N**. Accordingly, the red-black variety possesses the genetic formula **NR**. If we mate **NR** × **NR** fish, we obtain 50% **NN** black fish and 50% **RR** red fish. Only if heterozygous seminigra *Xiphophorus* with the genetic formula **Nn** or pure **NN** are mated with **RR** or **Nr**, are red-black Wiesbaden crossbreeds again produced.

## Frankfurt Crossbreed

As with all *Xiphophorus* crossbreeds, here too there are a number of ways to develop new color varieties. The Frankfurt crossbreed is named the Red Jet Swordtail in English, and was first introduced in the specialist literature in 1929, with an incorrect mating analysis, however.

Dr. Myron Gordon published a proposed cross in 1956 in an article in *Tropical Fish Hobbyist* magazine, which was and still is owned by his student, Dr. Herbert R. Axelrod. He introduced a red-black swordtail, which one must consider as identical to the Frankfurt crossbreed. The rear part of the bodies of the hybrids as well as the tail fin and sword exhibit a black coloration. The front part of the body as well as the remaining fins exhibit an intense red color. The line presented by Gordon originated from the mating of *Xiphophorus* wild species, namely *Xiphophorus helleri* females with *Xiphophorus cortezi* males. The *Xiphophorus helleri* female should, as far as possible, possess a red body ground color (for example, the red color variety from the Rio Atoyac, Mexico, or a tankbred red color variety of the *Xi-*

*Frankfurt crossbreed: a strain in which the fish are black posteriorly, red anteriorly; also known as the Red Jet Swordtail.*

This strain has several common names, among which are half black, red jet, and Frankfurt crossbreeed. Photo by Dr. H. R. Axelrod.

*"The line [Frankfurt crossbreed] presented by Gordon originated from the mating of* Xiphophorus *wild species, namely* Xiphophorus helleri *females with* Xiphophorus cortezi *males."*

*phophorus helleri* type). The *Xiphophorus cortezi* can be black-pied, but should, as far as possible, exhibit a band of black commas on the caudal peduncle.

In recent years the Frankfurt crossbreed has disappeared completely from our aquaria and thus awaits its renaissance. It is assumed that the described cross, like the red-black Wiesbaden cross, possesses the genetic formula **NR** and is therefore heterozygous.

The degeneration of various black factors into a black, cancerous condition represents a special problem for breeders and occurs very frequently with swordtail strains with black pigment.

*"Black pigment can never result from pure red and green fish."*

## Hamburg Crossbreed

As with the Frankfurt crossbreed, type *Xiphophorus helleri*, and with the Hamburg swordtail crossbreed as well, absolutely absurd breeding formulae circulate through the amateur literature. These false interpretations will not be reported on here. It remains only to be stated that the credit for the production of this quite attractive strain does not belong to those breeders who, in continuous selective breeding since the year 1912, have tried to develop the Hamburg crossbreed from matings of so-called red *Xiphophorus maculatus* males with green wild-colored *Xiphophorus* females.

The experienced breeder knows that black speckling is never masked in *Xiphophorus* and, therefore, must have been visible in the coloration of the starting material, relative to the discussed hybrid product. *Black pigmentation can never result from pure red and green fish.* The body colors of the Hamburg crossbreed are a deep blue-black with gleaming greenish scale edges. The breast is often

*Xiphophorus maculatus,* wild form from Rio Coatzacoalcos, Mexico. Photo by L. Wischnath.

The body colors of the Hamburg crossbreed are a deep blue-black with gleaming greenish scale edges. Photo by Dr. H. R. Axelrod.

light colored, while the tip of the snout is usually pink. All fins may be transparent. In recent years the well-known German breeder, Ranninger, has presented the Hamburg crossbreed with yellow fins at exhibitions. Especially impressive were the specimens with a high yellow dorsal fin.

The breeding of the Hamburg crossbreed proves to be a relatively simple matter, assuming that one uses the right wild fish. The most important thing is that *Xiphophorus maculatus* with the

A pair of Hamburg crossbreeds, male above, female below. Photo by R. Zukal.

A lyretail Hamburg crossbreed. Photo by A. Roth.

Facing page above: A Hamburg crossbreed in which the caudal fin of the male has streaks of black. Photo by A. Roth. Facing page below: A green swordtail with wild coloration. The spots are potential carcinomas. Photo by H.-J. Richter.

color gene *nigra* must be available. An article on a *Xiphophorus maculatus* population from the Rio Papaloapan with the color pattern *nigra-extended* has already been published with text and illustrations. This variety is particularly well suited for the re-creation of the Hamburg crossbreed when mated with a population of *Xiphophorus helleri* (it makes no difference which population is used). Useful fish already appear in the first generation.

Whether the fins will be transparent, yellow, or red can already be determined in the selection of the *Xiphophorus*

A pair of *Xiphophorus helleri.*

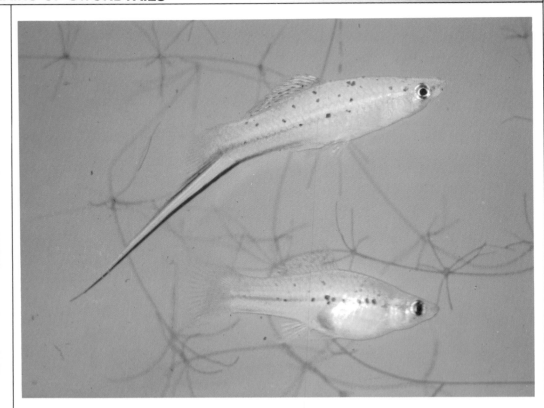

Although light colored, these fish are not albinos for they have black spotting and black eyes. Photo courtesy of Wardley Products.

*maculatus.* The *Xiphophorus maculatus* population from the Rio Papaloapan with the color pattern *nigra-extended* exhibits the above-mentioned fin colors in the wild.

## The Red Swordtail

The red swordtail is doubtless the only standard form that can always be purchased in the aquarium trade. Red is, however, not just red; today several color classes, such as orange-red, brick-red, and blood-red, can be distinguished. All of these red swordtails probably resulted from crosses with red races of *Xiphophorus maculatus.* In 1980, red *Xiphophorus helleri*

**Normally colored *Xiphophorus helleri* complete with black spots. Photo by H.-J. Richter.**

A common red swordtail pair, male below. Photo by A. Roth.

A male marigold twinbar lyretail (comet) swordtail. Photo by E. C. Taylor.

Although the dorsal fin is larger than normal in this lyretail, it is not a true hi-fin. Photo by Dr. J. Norton.

Many red swordtails have a platy mixture somewhere along the line as indicated by a shortened sword. Photo by Dr. H. R. Axelrod.

This is a magnificent specimen of a red lyretail swordtail.

*"To develop the wagtail, Myron Gordon from the New York Aquarium crossed a wild* Xiphophorus maculatus *with comet markings with a gold platy."*

A female marigold wag swordtail. Photo by E. C. Taylor.

were also collected for the first time in the wild. In addition to the body, the fins should also exhibit the same shade of color.

## The Wagtail Swordtail

The wagtail type made its appearance in the strains of *Xiphophorus* around 1940. To develop the wagtail, Myron Gordon from the New York Aquarium crossed a wild *Xiphophorus maculatus* with comet markings with a gold platy. In the following years it was also possible to transfer the wagtail markings to *Xiphophorus variatus* and *Xipho-*

A green wagtail swordtail male. Photo by K. Quitschau.

A female marigold wag lyretail swordtail. Photo by E. C. Taylor.

A male marigold wag swordtail. Photo by E. C. Taylor.

*phorus helleri*, and today it represents the most common type of fin marking. The rays of all fins are black colored, while the spaces between the rays remain largely free of melanin. Typical of the presence of the wagtail pattern is the black coloration of the upper and lower mandibles. Particularly rich in contrast is the red wagtail swordtail.

## The Arnold Factor

The wagtail type must not be confused with the Arnold factor. Here, too, the fins are black, but, according to Breider and Mom-

bour (1950), it is the fin membranes between the fin rays that are pigmented black. First bred by Riechers in Hamburg, the first black-finned *Xiphophorus helleri* reached the United States in 1936. In 1937, Arnold described these fish in the *Wochenschrift für Aquarien- und Terrariankunde*. The Arnold factor can already be recognized in day-old fishes. Three to five black spots are visible on the caudal peduncle, and the dorsal fin possesses melanin as well. With increasing age the black coloration of the

**A male marigold wag lyretail swordtail. Photo by E. C. Taylor.**

**A male red wag lyretail swordtail. Photo by E. C. Taylor.**

**A red wag lyretail swordtail female. Photo by E. C. Taylor.**

fins becomes more intense and assumes its ultimate appearance after two to three weeks. No specimens with either of these two markings have been observed in the wild.

## Albinos

Albino fishes are characterized by the lack of black body pigment. The red eyes are typical of albinos. The red of the eyes is caused by blood shining through and not, as one might assume, by a pigment. Since it is a question of an inheritable character here, it can be crossed into individual strains. During the early 1930s the first albino swordtails appeared in Germany and in the United States. With the type *Xiphophorus helleri* we recognize white, red, and yellowish albinos. The most attractive variety is the red, in which the red tint is particularly clean looking. Through crossbreeding we also find *Xiphophorus variatus* and *Xiphophorus maculatus* albinos.

All albinos place special demands on the breeder. Vitality and fertility are reduced in them. Through the lack of the black pigment in the eye they are sensitive to light and do not see as well, which makes finding food more difficult. In practice, it is therefore recommended to choose a location for the aquarium that is not too bright and to keep them only with others of their own kind. Should difficulties appear in breeding, one must quickly turn to half albinos (for more details see **Inheritance**). The inheritance of the albino gene occurs independently of the hereditary factors that are responsible for fin shape.

*"With the* Xiphophorus helleri *type we recognize white, red, and yellowish albinos."*

*Albinos: animals in which there is a lack of black pigments; red or pinkish eyes are typical.*

This complete moon blue platy has the Mickey Mouse design at the caudal base. The male also has a red dorsal, making it a very attractive strain. Photo by A. Roth.

# STANDARD STRAINS OF PLATIES

## *MACULATUS* TYPE

As far as possible, the standard should correspond to the wild form *Xiphophorus maculatus* in form and size.

**Total length:** females 4 to 5 centimeters, males 3 to 4 centimeters.

**Ground colors of body:** Wild-colored, albino, and golden.

**Color pattern:** The color pattern should be intense; the markings may not merge into one another. The caudal peduncle may exhibit markings.

**Fin colors:** As in Helleri type.

**Fin forms:** 1. Normal finned.
               2. Highfin (flag form).
               3. Brush tail and pointed tail.
               4. Lyretail.

1. The fin form should correspond to that of the wild type *Xiphophorus maculatus*.
2. Only the flag form is desired; otherwise see *variatus* type.
3. and 4. Correspond to *variatus*.

## The Bleeding Heart Platy

In 1939, in the Rio Jamapa region near Veracruz in Mexico, Gordon collected a *Xiphophorus maculatus* with a red throat. He gave this color pattern the name *rubythroat*. Hnilicka was able to collect the same color variety in 1981 in the Rio Papaloapan. In the journal *Animal Kingdom* from 1951 Gordon described how he bred the Bleeding Heart Platy. He presented a combina-

A gold comet platy (upper fish) and a red topsail platy, both males. Photo by L. Wischnath.

*"In 1939, in the Rio Jamapa region near Veracruz in Mexico, Gordon collected a* Xiphophorus maculatus *with a red throat."*

A female tuxedo platy exhibiting a well-developed brushtail. Photo by G. Entlinger.

Two female pearl albino platies, the pearly scales resembling those of the pearl-scaled goldfish. Photo by Dr. J. Norton.

True albino platies are not as common as albino swordtails. Photo of a female pearl albino platy by Dr. J. Norton.

A female brushtail platy. The extended abdomen indicates that she has developing embryos within her. Photo by A. Kochetov.

This is a prizewinning albino swordtail. Photo by Dr. H. Grier.

It can easily be seen why this strain is called the bleeding heart platy. Photo by A. van den Nieuwenhuizen.

The first bleeding heart platies were exhibited at the New York Zoo. Photo by Dr. H. R. Axelrod.

*Bleeding heart platy: one in which red color is concentrated at the breast, looking like blood flowing from a wound.*

tion of a strain and a wild form. The strain was a so-called White Ghost Platy; the wild form was the *Xiphophorus maculatus* with *rubythroat*. The first Bleeding Heart Platies were exhibited in 1948 in the aquarium of the New York Zoo. They reached Germany in 1949. Gordon regretted that only males exhibited the color pattern, and believed that it was only a matter of time before females would also display this pattern, which looks like blood flowing from a wound. This would be entirely conceivable by breeding this variety with southern stocks of *Xiphophorus maculatus*, such as populations from the Belize River. Since Bleeding Heart Platies have now almost disappeared from aquaria again, here is a fascinating opportunity for the dedicated breeder. There are also a number of other ornamental varieties that, based on their appearance, could have been derived from the Bleeding Heart Platy.

## The Red Maculatus (Red Platy, Coral Platy)

Just as with the red strain of *Xiphophorus helleri*, the red coloration in the varieties of *Xiphophorus maculatus* should also be grouped in different color classes. In this case two classes are advisable: color class 1 includes the Coral or Blood Red Platies; all other shades of red, including orange, brick red, etc., are placed in color class 2.

In Coral Platies, besides the bright red color, the reddish-colored eye ring is conspicuous.

A red twinbar platy female. Photo by Dr. H. Grier.

*". . . fish that exhibit stunted growth or poor color quality should never be purchased."*

The pattern in this red platy is not very clear. It may be an ax-head or a very poor Mickey Mouse. Photo by Dr. H. R. Axelrod.

The fins are also red. Recently, however, the quality and vitality of the beautiful Coral Platies have regrettably suffered greatly. To blame for this evil is above all the high-volume breeding of this fish all over the world. Therefore, fish that exhibit stunted growth or poor color quality should never be purchased. Strains that still possess a distinct so-called inner sword are unsuitable for our efforts in breeding standard forms.

This male salt-and-pepper platy is another prize winner. Photo by Dr. H. Grier.

A pair of red platies, male above. Photo by B. Kahl.

## The Salt-and-pepper Maculatus (Salt-and-pepper Platy)

According to Gordon, the salt-and-pepper color pattern is supposed to have been derived from wild forms of *Xiphophorus maculatus* from Honduras. The entire body of the fish is covered with innumerable black spots, while the background appears white. Males are more heavily spotted than females, particularly in the rear part of the caudal peduncle. All of the fins may be sprinkled with black. Some fish also exhibit a red coloration or various shades of yellow in the fins. In recent years the Salt-and-pepper Platy has unfortunately completely disappeared from fanciers' aquaria.

The Orange-spot Platy is another very interesting strain. The ground color of the body consists of orange-red colored scales with a lighter ventral side. The upper part of the back exhibits numerous black spots, which are more conspicuous in males than in females. The tail fin is either intense red or marked with black. The male's dorsal fin has a pattern of black spots on a red background; the female's is a uniform red color.

The red strains need high temperatures and therefore should not be kept below 25° C.

## The Golden Maculatus (Gold Platy)

The Gold Platy was described in the year 1916 in the aquarium literature. According to Kammerzell, several fish with a yellow ground color of the body were found among the offspring of the strain *Xiphophorus maculatus* with the *rubra* color gene. Apparently, this strain was lost in the following years. In 1920, Struve again described platies with a yellow ground color of the body and coined the name Gold Platy.

In 1931, Gordon was able to prove that the gold coloration resulted from the reduction of the black melanin and that it exhibits recessive autosomal inheritance. Today the most diverse sports of the Gold Platy are found in our aquaria, of which only a few will be mentioned here. The true golden platies are divided into two color classes.

To color class 1 belong fishes with an intense yellow-gold coloration of the body. Fish with a whitish-gold coloration are placed in color class 2. It is assumed that whitish-gold and yellow-gold are inherited through different genes.

Impressive above all is the yellow-gold strain with pale-yellow tinged fins. A variety with a red-colored dorsal fin also occurs. Other very attractive varie-

This young female bleeding heart platy has faded due to fright. Photo by Dr. J. Norton.

This colorful strain of platy was developed in Miami in 1963. Photo by Dr. H. R. Axelrod.

The complete moon or Mickey Mouse pattern on the tail is clear in these gold platies.

First generation hybrids, *X. maculatus* X *X. milleri*. Photo by K. Kallman.

Rio Grijalva platies (*X. maculatus*) with weak spotted dorsal character. Photo by K. Kallman.

*Xiphophorus maculatus* from Rio Coatzacoalcos. Photo courtesy N. Y. Zoological Society.

A pair of red moon platies, *Xiphophorus maculatus*. Photo by Dr. H. R. Axelrod.

ties of the Gold Platy are the Moon Platy, the Comet Platy, the Mickey Mouse Platy and the Crescent Platy. They differ only in the markings of the caudal peduncle (see *Tail Patterns*).

## The Nigra Maculatus (Black Platy)

The name Nigra Maculatus refers to the more or less extensive black coloration on the sides of the body. The nigra color gene was introduced into fish genetics in 1922 by Bellamy. Various *Xiphophorus maculatus* occur in the wild, which, de-

A sunburst twinbar or comet platy. Photo by Dr. H. Grier.

A pair of common red platies. Photo by R. Zukal.

A small group
of gold Mickey
Mouse platies
with red
dorsals. Photo
by B. Kahl.

Blood red wag
platies. Photo
by B. Kahl.

Male bleeding heart hi-fin platy. It even has a Mickey Mouse pattern. Photo by Dr. J. Norton.

A pair of gold comet platies. Photo by Dr. H. R. Axelrod.

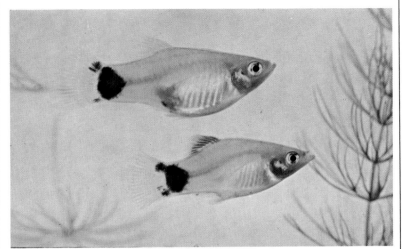

A pair of gold crescent moons with a weak Mickey Mouse pattern. Photo by Dr. H. R. Axelrod.

A pair of black variatus platies, male above, female below. Photo by Dr. H. R. Axelrod.

A gold comet female platy with a red dorsal fin. Photo by S. Frank.

pending on the population, possess other colors in addition to the black factor.

Wild forms from Rio Papaloapan, Mexico, were already discussed. Populations with the nigra color gene are known from Rio Usumacinta, Rio Grijalva, and Rio Coatzacoalcos, as well as the river systems of Honduras and Belize. All vary considerably in the degree to which the black coloration is expressed and in fin pigmentation. In the southern *Xiphophorus maculatus*, the genes for the nigra factor are located on the Z sex chromosomes. Consequently, both sexes exhibit the black coloration. In the platies from the Rio Papaloapan, the black factor lies on the Y sex chromosome. Here only males exhibit the black coloration of the body, while females are a uniform gray.

Aquarists have succeeded in altering various *Xiphophorus maculatus* wild forms for the aquarium hobby; for example, there are fishes with intense black markings and a red or yellow dorsal fin, whereas the tail fin generally remains transparent. Perhaps it will also be possible before long to breed fishes with red on the tail fin as well. A cross with the red-yellow *Xiphophorus variatus* could be useful for this purpose. The Nigra Maculatus is not all that easy to breed, since females produce far fewer young than is normally expected with other *Xiphophorus* strains. A varied diet and higher water temperatures could perhaps change this.

Fancy platies developed from recent crosses between hi-fin swordtails, hi-fin variatus, Nubian variatus, and red wag platies. Photo by Dr. H. R. Axelrod.

A pair of red tuxedo platies. Photo by Andre Roth.

Red tuxedo platies with the black less well developed. Photo by Dr. H. R. Axelrod.

Blue mirror platies are quite impressive. This character is being worked into other strains. Photo by Dr. H. R. Axelrod.

## The Mirror Maculatus (Mirror Platy)

The most diverse varieties have already been kept in aquaria under the name Mirror Maculatus. The basis for this is a color pattern which, like salt-and-pepper and nigra, also occurs in the wild.

The mirrored effect of the scales could in part be intensified through crossing in the most varied *Xiphophorus maculatus* populations. The so-called Blue Mirror Platies, in which the ground color can be gray or yellow, are impressive. The refinement of the Mirror Maculatus has not yet been pursued intensively. It is to be hoped that new varieties will be bred in the coming years.

## The Soot Maculatus (Soot Platy)

The so-called *fuliginosus* color gene determines the black coloration of the Soot Platy. This color gene was first mentioned by Kosswig in 1938. According to Gordon, the gene is supposed to have originated in 1955 as a result of a mutation in domesticated *Xiphophorus maculatus*. The following description of the coloration was published in 1975 by Wolf and Anders: Fuliginosus fishes are more or less black colored on the entire body up to but excluding the breast, which gives the impression of an irregular layer of soot covering the fish. In addition to the body, the unpaired fins are also colored.

In contrast to the nigra color gene, newborn Soot Platies already have an intense black coloration of the body and the dorsal and tail fins. By means of crossing experiments, Kosswig

Red iridescent
Mickey Mouse
platies. Photo
by B. Kahl.

Blue crescent
mirror platy.
Photo by Dr. H.
R. Axelrod.

An attractive male gold tuxedo platy. Photo by S. Frank.

Two variations in platy strains. Upper fish is a sunburst twinbar platy; lower fish is a peppermint twinbar sword. Photos courtesy FTFFA.

was able to prove that the fuliginosus color is inherited through a dominant gene on the **Z** chromosome.

Specimens of the Soot Maculatus with a red-colored dorsal fin occasionally occur. If these are crossed with *Xiphophorus helleri*, the pigmentation of the black factor is intensified. In fry, this degeneration of the black pigment cells can lead to the formation of melanomas and thus to premature death. The Soot Maculatus is rarely kept in aquaria today. It has been supplanted by the similar Nigra Maculatus.

# STANDARD STRAINS OF *XIPHOPHORUS VARIATUS*

## *VARIATUS* TYPE

These standard forms should resemble the wild *Xiphophorus variatus* in form and size.

**Total length:** males 4 to 5 centimeters, females 4 to 6 centimeters.

**Ground colors of body:** wild-colored, red, albino, and golden.

**Color patterns:** The colors should be as intense as possible. The markings must be clearly set off from one another. In the Parrot Variatus, on the other hand, the colors should, as far as possible, merge with one another.

Markings on the caudal peduncle are undesirable.

**Fin colors:** black, red, yellow, or colorless; otherwise, as the *helleri* type.

Fin forms: 1. Normal fin.
2. Highfin (flag form, veil form).
3. Brush tail and pointed tail.
4. Lyretail.

A pair of marigold platies, male below. Photo by Andre Roth.

A pair of black-and-gold platies. Photo by Dr. H. R. Axelrod.

165

1. The normal fin should correspond to the wild *Xiphophorus variatus* in fin form. No trace of a sword may be visible.

2. In the flag form all of the fin rays of the dorsal fin are elongated twofold to threefold; in the veil form they are elongated threefold to fourfold. The top margin of the highfin should be as straight as possible. Also permitted, however, are fish, above all females, in which the first fin ray is extended to a point.

3. In the brush tail the median fin rays of the tail fin are elongated about twofold and are almost parallel to one another. In the pointed tail, the median fin rays again are elongated twofold, but they taper to a point. The tail fin resembles the point of a spear. Both tail forms are the same in both sexes.

4. Resembles the *helleri* type in appearance, but without the suggestion of a sword in males.

**Top: Hi-fin sunburst variatus male. Above: Normal finned rainbow variatus male. Photos courtesy FTFFA.**

**Two male sunburst variatus platies. Photo by A. van den Nieuwenhuizen.**

## The Golden Variatus and Yellow-red Variatus

With *Xiphophorus variatus* we can observe quite a few yellow varieties. The yellow is usually combined with red. The Marsh-marigold Variatus and the Marigold Variatus are particularly popular. Both were not bred until recently. The repeated crossing of *Xiphophorus variatus* with the Golden Helleri could have led to these beautiful color varieties. In the Marsh-marigold Variatus, the female and male are the same color; in the Marigold Variatus the female is pure yellow.

Yellow-red Variatus were already bred from the wild form at the beginning of the 1930s. Since the males vary a great deal, they were good subjects for experimentation. The high fin was also crossed into some strains of the

Top: Rainbow variatus male without any indication of sword. Above: Rainbow variatus with indication of sword showing hybrid origin. Photos courtesy FTFFA.

A male marigold variatus. Photo by H.-J. Richter.

167

Yellow-red Variatus. There is also a Bleeding Heart or Blushing Marigold developed in Florida in the mid-1960s.

## The Hawaiian Variatus

The Hawaiian Variatus is also known as the Black Variatus. Mombour presented this interesting strain in the *Deutschen Aquarien- und Terrarienzeitschrift* of 1949. The breeder, Wrobel, in Wiesbaden succeeded in breeding a Black Variatus through systematic crossing and selection. According to Mombour, the fuliginosus color gene of *Xiphophorus maculatus* is supposed to be responsible for the black col-

**A pair of sunburst platies, male below. Photo by M. Gilroy.**

*Hawaiian variatus: a strain in which the body is black but the ventral side is white; the tail fin is bright red and the dorsal fin is yellow.*

**Three male *Xiphophorus variatus*. Photo by B. Kahl.**

Two male hi-fin variatus platies, blue strain above, gold strain below. Photo by Dr. H. R. Axelrod.

A female wagtail variatus platy showing the brushtail character. Photo by G. Entlinger.

oration. Through repeated back-crossing it was possible to transfer this gene of the Soot Platy to the wild-colored variatus. After 1960 the black strain underwent further change and today is named the Hawaiian Variatus. The Hawaiian Variatus is characterized by a bright red tail fin and a yellow-colored dorsal fin.

The Hawaiian variatus is a black fish with a red tail and yellow dorsal fin.

The body is black and the ventral side is light. For the preservation and further breeding of this beautiful variety, Klein the breeder in Frankfurt, deserves special mention. It is interesting that the fuliginosus color gene in the *variatus* type apparently is protected against malignant degeneration. So far no tumor development has been observed. Nevertheless, in many cases the development of the Hawaiian Variatus has not proved easy. Keeping them at cooler temperatures seems to promote the well-being of the fish. The most beautiful males usually are not fully colored until they are two years old. The Highfin Hawaiian Variatus is particularly impressive looking.

## The Parrot Variatus

The Parrot Variatus is a beautifully colored fish. It is found in almost every conceivable color combination. The more colorful it is, the higher its scores will be in competitive aquarium exhibitions. At least three colors should be observed on the body. Particularly striking are black-spotted fish with iridescent blue and red scales in the central part of the body.

## The Tuxedo Variatus

In recent years numerous strains have appeared in the aquarium trade under the name *tuxedo*. Characteristic of the tuxedo coloration is that it extends extensively over the middle of the body. The black pigmentation appears to be derivable from the Wiesbaden cross as well as the Hamburg cross. The rest of the body may be green, yellow, or red.

The dorsal and caudal fins are usually tinged with red, but fish with black fins (Arnold factor?) have also been bred. It remains to be seen whether it can gain acceptance as a standard. Tuxedo-like *maculatus* and *helleri* have also been bred by Dr. Myron Gordon in New York many years ago.

A hi-fin Hawaiian variatus platy. Photo by Dr. J. Norton.

Two male Hawaiian variatus. Photo by A. van den Nieuwenhuizen.

A male parrot variatus. Photo by H.-J. Richter.

Two male parrot variatus. Photo by Dr. H. Grier.

Two views of a tank full of marigold platies. Photo by Dr. H. R. Axelrod.

172

Black variatus platies. Photo by Dr. H. R. Axelrod.

Red-tailed salt-and-pepper platies.

A hi-fin marigold variatus male. Photo by E. C. Taylor.

Two males and a female variatus platy.

Parrot platies with the large "Simpson fin," a somewhat larger body, and more intense coloration. Photo by B. Kahl.

# TAIL PATTERNS

In numerous representatives of the genus *Xiphophorus*, different patterns are found on the base of the tail and the tail fin, which are referred to as tail patterns. The black coloration is shared by all of these patterns. The greatest diversity of forms is found in *Xiphophorus maculatus* and *Xiphophorus variatus*. Since in selective breeding we only deal with *Xiphophorus helleri*, *Xiphophorus maculatus*, and *Xiphophorus variatus*, the description of tail patterns is limited to these forms.

## Tail Patterns of *Xiphophorus maculatus*

### 1. Ax-head.

According to Rosen (1960), ax-head is an ax-head-like pattern of the micro-melanophores, which represents the front element of the complete crescent pattern. It is said to be very rare. Nothing is known about its genetic basis.

### 2. Comet.

In the comet pattern two narrow black stripes extend on the upper and lower edges of the tail fin. If comet specimens are crossed with various domesticated strains of *Xiphophorus maculatus* or wild or domesticated *Xiphophorus helleri*, then comet is intensified to a pattern called *wagtail* (see *wagtail* under *Xiphophorus helleri*).

### 3. Complete crescent.

Complete crescent consists of two elements: a crescent-shaped part in the rear and an ax-head-like spot in front.

Blue mirror platies with a complete crescent tail pattern. Photo by B. Kahl.

A prize-winning female gold flame twinbar (comet) platy. Photo by Dr. H. Grier.

175

Twinbar or comet gold platies. Photo by M. F. Roberts.

Red wagtail platies, female below. Photo by B. Kahl.

A long-finned platy with the cut crescent tail pattern.

*Mickey Mouse tail pattern: consists of a large black spot (moon) and two smaller spots (satellites). Also known as complete moon.*

### 4. Cut crescent.

In the cut crescent, the central part of the crescent is lacking. Only two spots remain, above and below on the base of the tail fin.

### 5. Lower comet.

This is a pattern that consists only of the lower part of the comet pattern.

### 6. Lower cut crescent.

This rare pattern was mentioned only by Rosen (1960). In it only the lower spot of the cut crescent is expressed.

### 7. Moon.

According to Gordon's schematic diagrams, the moon pattern is the same as complete moon without the satellites.

### 8. Complete moon.

This pattern consists of three elements: the actual moon and two satellites. The moon is a large, roundish spot, the rear edge of which lies in front of the beginning of the tail fin rays. Sometimes called "Mickey Mouse."

### 9. One spot.

The one spot pattern is located in the rear part of the caudal peduncle. Its rear border lies just in front of the beginning of the tail fin rays. A similar pattern is called *dot*. It is scarcely distinguishable from one spot in appearance.

**A pair of complete moon platies, otherwise known as the Mickey Mouse tail pattern. Photo by B. Kahl.**

A pair of blue platies with the complete moon or Mickey Mouse tail pattern. Photo by M. Gilroy.

**10. Twin spot.**

This pattern consists of two spots, which are located symmetrically in the caudal peduncle along the long axis of the body. The rear edges of both spots coincide with the rear boundry of the rudiments of the muscle of the tail fin. There is no distinct boundry in the forward direction.

**11. Upper comet.**

Upper comet consists of only the upper part of the comet pattern. This pattern occurs very rarely.

**12. Upper cut crescent.**

In this pattern only the upper spot of cut crescent is present.

## Tail Patterns of *Xiphophorus variatus*

**1. Crescent.**

In form and composition, the crescent pattern of *Xiphophorus variatus* resembles that of *Xiphophorus maculatus*.

**2. Cut crescent.**

This pattern consists of two spots, which are located symmetrically to the long axis of the tail fin. The front and rear limits

A gold comet or modified twinbar gold platy male. Photo by M. F. Roberts.

This appears to be a red-finned blue topsail platy with a twin spot tail pattern, but it is very close to the cut crescent pattern. Photo by Dr. J. Norton.

A pair of red wag platies. Photo by A. Roth.

of the two spots are not in the same place in all specimens. Frequently both spots extend to the rear beyond the limit of the crescent pattern. Both spots can also extend forward past the limit of the crescent pattern.

3. **Peduncular spot.**

In the old nomenclature, *peduncular spot* was called *one spot* or *moon*. The new name for the pattern was chosen because it differs from the *moon* and *one*

A male bleeding heart hi-fin platy. Photo by G. Takeshita.

The peduncular spots are sometimes obscure.

A pair of ruby yellowtail variatus platies. Photo by Dr. H. R. Axelrod.

*spot* patterns of *Xiphophorus maculatus.*

4. **Upper cut crescent.**

In contrast to the cut crescent pattern, in upper cut crescent only one spot in the upper caudal peduncle region is present.

## Tail patterns of *Xiphophorus helleri*

In the wild populations of *Xiphophorus helleri*, not a single pattern of the caudal peduncle region or the tail fin has been found so far. The entire *Xiphophorus helleri* complex has only one caudal peduncle pattern.

A trio of marigold variatus platies. Photo by Dr. H. R. Axelrod.

Two male blue variatus platies with crescent tail patterns. Photo by Dr. C. D. Zander.

A gold moon male platy with two poorly developed "satellites." Photo by S. Frank.

This is found in *Xiphophorus signum* and is called *grave*. Those patterns that occur in *Xiphophorus helleri* strains originally came from other *Xiphophorus* species. In all three types that are used for selective breeding, *helleri*, *maculatus*, and *variatus*, in addition to the described tail patterns new combinations that result from crossing can occur. The patterns that were developed through selective breeding

A cut crescent caudal pattern in a gold variatus.

must be treated separately. At the moment too little material exists for their description.

## Other *Xiphophorus* Strains

In addition to the strains presented here, other color and form varieties are occasionally found in the aquarium trade. Generally, however, these fish are held in community tanks, so that it cannot be determined whether or not they are pure strains. With livebearers only attractive fishes can be easily sold, thus the colors red and black predominate. The Southeast Asian breeders, in particular, continually try to attract the attention of their buyers with new varieties in order to expand the market for their fishes. Besides conspicuous colors, these fishes often have fanciful names.

Furthermore, translations of English or American names often lead to difficulties in comprehension. This is usually reflected in different spellings of the names. For this reason photographs of strains are of the greatest importance, for only they permit comparisons and make clear what is concealed behind the individual names. For the serious *Xiphophorus* breeder, the attraction lies in the purchase of new strains as well as in the preservation and improvement of existing stocks. Since virtually every aquarist in the course of his participation in the aquarium hobby has kept or bred *Xiphophorus* strains, he is familiar with many strains and varieties. Because of the diversity of colors and forms, the members of the genus *Xiphophorus* contribute a great deal to the enrichment of our aquaria.

A neon lyretail swordtail female. Photo by E. C. Taylor.

A neon lyretail swordtail male. Photo by E. C. Taylor.

A gold flame twinbar (comet) swordtail. Photo by E. C. Taylor.

A pineapple twinbar (comet) swordtail. Photo by E. C. Taylor.

# FISH DISEASES AFFECTING *XIPHOPHORUS*

In the care and breeding of the valuable species of the genus *Xiphophorus*, a variety of diseases can lead to substantial losses or even the complete destruction of a stock. As a result of the excellent remedies that have been developed, veterinary medicine is now largely in the position to effect a cure if the disease is recognized in time and the right medicine is used. Understandably, the different remedies produced by individual manufacturers cannot be named here. The most common fish diseases and their symptoms will, however, be explained.

A female swordtail exhibiting extreme emaciation. Photo by Ruda Zukal.

## Description of Disease

*Achyla* and *Saprolegnia* (fungus).

*Costia* (skin slime).

Fin rot.

Fin clamping.

*Dactylogyrus* and *Gyrodactylus* (skin flukes of freshwater fishes).
*Ichthyophthirius multifiliis* (Ich).

Fungusing of clutch.

Mouth fungus.

*Oodinium pillularis* (velvet).

## Symptoms

Cottony, white areas form on wounds and skin injuries.

Mottled and gray clouding of the skin together with emaciation.

Whitish deposits form on the fins. The tips of the fins become ragged and, if treatment is not started in time, the entire fin can be lost.

Signs of extreme discomfort; secondary manifestation of various diseases and internal and external parasites of various kinds.

Gills redden and become congested with slime.

First a few small white spots appear on the fins and body. Later the whole body is covered.

White or gray fungus infestation of fish eggs or fry.

Fungus infestation on mouth of fish. Usually the result of an injury. Very common with livebearing toothcarps.

Similar in appearance to *Ichthyophthirius multifiliis*, except the spots are smaller. In heavy infestations a grayish white deposit forms.

# INDEX OF LITERATURE FOR
## *XIPHOPHORUS*

## WILD FORMS

Kallmann, K. D. (1964): Genetics of Tissue Transplantation in Isolated Platyfish Populations. *Copeia* (3): pp. 513–522.

Meek, S. E. (1904): The Fresh-water fishes of Mexico north of the Isthmus of Tehuantepec. *Field Columbian Mus. Publ., Zool. Ser.,* vol 5: pp. 1–252.

Meyer, M. K. and L. Wischnath (1981): *Xiphophorus kosszanderi* und *Xiphophorus roseni. TI* 56, p. 37.

Meyer, M. K. (1983): *Xiphophorus* Hybriden aus Nordmexico, mit einer Revision der Taxa *Xiphophorus kosszanderi* und *Xiphophorus roseni.* Mit einer brieflichen Mitteilung von Dr. S. Contreras-Balderas zur Problematik der *Xiphophorus*-Hybridisierung von Monterrey. *Zool. Abh. Mus. Tierk.,* Dresden, 38 (16): pp. 285–291.

Radda, A. C. (1980): Synopsis der Gattung *Xiphophorus* Heckel. *Aquaria,* 27: pp. 39–44.

Rosen, D. E. and K. D. Kallmann (1969): A new fish of the genus *Xiphophorus* from Guatemala, with remarks on the taxonomy of endemic forms. *Amer. Mus. Novitates* #2379: pp 1–29.

Wischnath, L. (1983): Les Formes Sauvages du Porte-Epee. *Aquarama* 74, pp. 22–25; and *Aquarama* 76, pp. 14–15 and 70.

Wischnath, L. (1987): Stalking the Wild Swordtails. *Tropical Fish Hobbyist,* no. 11: pp. 86–90.

Wischnath, L. (1988): Color Varieties of *Xiphophorus helleri. Tropical Fish Hobbyist,* no. 1: pp. 86–90.

Zander, C. D. (1967): Ökologische and morphologische Beiträge zur Systematik und geografischen Verbreitung der Gattung *Xiphophorus. Mitt. Hamburg. Zool. Mus. Inst.,* 64: pp. 87–125.

## STRAINS

Anders, F., Klinke K., and U. Vielkind (1972): Genregulation und Differenzierung im Melanomsystem der Zahnkärpflinge. *Biologie in unserer Zeit,* 2: pp. 35–36.

Arnold, J. P. (1912): Über Melanismus bei den lebendgebärenden Zahnkarpfen. *Wochenschrift für Aquarien- und Terrarienkunde,* 9: pp. 377–379.

Becker-Carus, C. (1965): Untersuchungen zur Phänogenese von Melanophorenmustern bei Zahnkarpfen. *Zeitschrift für wissenschaftliche Zoologie,* A 172: pp. 37–103.

Bellamy, A. W. (1922): Breeding Experiments with the Viviparous Teleosts, *Xiphophorus helleri* and *Platypoecilus maculatus. The Anatomical Record,* 23: pp. 98–99.

Breider, H. (1934): Die Besamungsfolge bei den lebendgebärenden Zahnkarpfen. *Zoologischer Anzeiger,* 106: pp. 131–132.

Breider, H. (1935): Albino-Schwertfische. *Wochenschrift für Aquarien- und Terrarienkunde*, 32: pp. 131-132.

Breider, H. (1950): Vom Arnold-Helleri und Wagtail-Platy. *Deutsche Aquarien- und Terrarien-Zeitschrift*, 3: pp. 101–103.

Foerster, W. und F. Anders (1977): Zytogenetischer Vergleich der Karyotypen verschiedener Rassen und Arten lebendgebärender Zahnkarpfen der Gattung *Xiphophorus*. *Zool. Anz.*, 198: pp. 167–177.

Frank, D. (1964): Vergleichende Verhaltensstudien an lebendgebärenden Zahnkarpfen der Gattung *Xiphophorus*. *Zoologische Jahrbücher für allgemeine Zoologie und Physiologie*, 71: pp. 117–170.

Gordon, M. (1942): Mortality of Albino Embryos and Aberrant Mendelian Ratios in Certain Broods of *Xiphophorus helleri*. *Zoologica* (New York) 27: pp. 73–74.

Gordon, M. (1951): How the Bleeding-heart Platy was invented. *Animal Kingdom*, 54: pp. 43–46.

Kallmann, K. D. (1965): Genetics and Geography of Sex Determination in the Poeciliid Fish, *Xiphophorus maculatus*. *Zoologica* (New York) 50: pp. 151–190.

Kammerzell, F. (1918): Über Gelbfärbung bei *Platypoecilus maculatus*, rote Varietät. *Wochenschrift für Aquarien- und Terrarienkunde*, 15: pp. 115–116.

Kosswig, C. (1930): Die Geschlechtsbestimmung bei Bastarden von *Xiphophorus helleri* und *Platypoecilus maculatus* und deren Nachkommen. *Zeitschrift für induktive Abstammungs- und Vererbungslehre*. 54: pp. 263–267.

Kosswig, C. (1935): Über Albinismus bei Fischen. *Zoologischer Anzeiger*, 110: pp. 41–47.

Krasper, E. (1921): Ein neuer *Xiphophorus*, der gelbe Schwertträger. *Blätter für Aquarien- und Terrarienkunde*, 32: pp. 18–19.

Schreitmüller, W. (1934): Totalalbinos von *Xiphophorus helleri* Heckel und xanthoristische *Lebistes reticulatus* Peters. *Zool. Anz.* 106: pp. 333–334.

Zander, C. D. (1961): Künstliche Befruchtung bei lebendgebärenden Zahnkarpfen. *Zool. Anz.* 166: pp. 81–87.

## BOOKS AND PAMPHLETS

Axelrod, H. R., Burgess, W. E., Pronek, N., and J. G. Walls. *Dr. Axelrod's Atlas*, Third Edition. T. F. H. Publications, Inc., 1989.

Axelrod, H. R. and M. Gordon: *Swordtails for the advanced hobbyist*. T. F. H. Publications, Inc., 1968.

Brembach, M.: *Lebendgebärende Fische im Aquarium*. Kosmos Verlag, Reihe: Das Vivarium. Stuttgart, 1979.

Frank, S.: *Das grosse Bildlexikon der Fische*. Bertelsmann Verlag, Vienna, 1975.

Gärtner, G.: *Zahnkarpfen—die Lebendgebärenden im Aquarium*. Ulmer Verlag, Stuttgart, 1981.

Jacobs, K.: *Die Lebendgebärenden Fische des Süsswassers*. Harri Deutsch Verlag, Frankfurt/-Zurich, 1969.

Meyer, M. K. and Wischnath, L.: *Svärdbärare och Platy*. Tidskriften Akvariet, Göteborg, 1983.

Meyer, M. K., Wischnath, L., and W. Foerster: *Lebendgebärende Zierfische, Arten der Welt*. Mergus Verlag, Melle, 1985.

Plöger-Brembach, K.: *Lebendgebärende*. Kernen Verlag, Stuttgart, 1982.

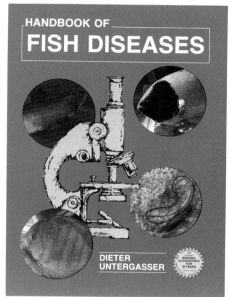

# Index

# SWORDTAILS
# AND PLATIES

Dr. Herbert R. Axelrod
Mr. Lothar Wischnath